MAKING THE ~~MOST~~ NEW TECHNOLOGY

A How-To-Do-It Manual

Kathleen R.T. Imhoff

HOW-TO-DO-IT MANUALS FOR LIBRARIANS

NUMBER 64

NEAL-SCHUMAN PUBLISHERS, INC.
New York, London

Published by Neal-Schuman Publishers, Inc.
100 Varick Street
New York, NY 10013

Copyright © 1996 by Kathleen R.T. Imhoff

Printed and bound in the United States of America.

Library of Congress Cataloging-in-Publication Data

Imhoff, Kathleen.
    Making the most of new technology : a how-to-do-it manual for
librarians / by Kathleen R.T. Imhoff.
        p.   cm — (How to do it manual for librarians ; 64)
    Includes bibliographical references and index.
    ISBN 1-55570-232-5 (alk. paper)
    1. Libraries—United States—Data processing.   I. Title.
II. Series: How-to-do-it manual ; no. 64.
Z678.9.A4U645   1996
025'.00285—dc20   96-2319

ACKNOWLEDGEMENTS

This book would not have been possible without the help of the following people: my Nintendo-age, sounding-board children, Eliot and Ethan; my patient, supportive husband, Clement; and my friend, Mary Hedrick. Special thanks to Larry Knauff for the first part of Chapter Two; he is a Victor with Vision.

CONTENTS

ILLUSTRATIONS

PREFACE

We live in the rapids of change. The white waters carry us quickly on; we cannot slow down the changes coming to our culture, our society, our families, ourselves. But we do have a choice: we can learn to enjoy turbulence rather than be overwhelmed by it.
—Robert Theobald

Visualize yourself in a small kayak—alone, without a life jacket, and swept around a sharp bend into unexpected rapids. What do you see around that bend? More white water, rocks, and cold water splashing into the wobbly raft, possibly capsized, or calm, blue, warm, reflecting water with pine trees outlined against the horizon?

If we had a choice, all but the most adventurous of us would pick the latter or at least add a life jacket to the former. Every day in libraries we make or avoid making choices that might not be as dramatic as the next bend on a dangerous, rushing river trip but nonetheless create technostress, technofear, amd automation anxiety which make it difficult to move ahead in the new world of technology.

I decided to write *Making the Most of New Technology* so that readers could understand the continuous process of introducing technology in order to improve library services to users. Whether the change is introducing microform publishing or electronic publishing, all types of libraries can benefit from the process of exploring new products and services, evaluating whether or not they could be advantageous to the library's specific situation, and coming to understand that technology offers both challenges and opportunities.

Virtual reality, multimedia, 3DOMO, CD-ROM, CDR, DVD, and WWW—will these technologies change the library? *Making the Most of New Technology* will help librarians understand some of the changes coming to the world that will affect libraries and information delivery. *Making the Most of New Technology* provides guidelines for preparing a technology plan, coping tools, and an in-depth look at factors that will affect dealing with change and technological planning. The book explores possible roles a library could choose in the future and explains the technologies which could be used. The Idea Analysis Worksheet in Chapter 2 teaches how to plan for technology change, without tears, and outlines new opportunities for you to improve services to your client group.

Technological change appears to be bombarding us from every newspaper, television advertisement, and news magazine. Headlines and lead stories tout new machines, new home delivery systems, and cheaper, more powerful equipment. Buy, buy, buy, more, more, more of the new, new, new. Yet many libraries of all types have less, less, less to meet more, more, more demands for service. How do we manage to plan and give service while at the same time managing uncertainties concerning the expenditures of the scarce resources? How do we learn to enjoy turbulence? Is it even possible? If you are the only staff person in a small library, where do you find the time to sort through the converging technologies? How can you guess which will work best for your patrons? How can you find time to weigh the alternatives?

Some media organizations predict that everyone shortly will have met all their information, entertainment, recreation, and shopping needs from a comfortable, well-worn arm chair in the living room. Nathan Myhrvold, chief of advanced technology for Microsoft says of the Microsoft Network, "It will let anyone with a PC hooked to a phone line find the answer to virtually any question, identify, and communicate with like-minded people all over the country, transact household business and entertain himself and his family, all without ever budging from the den."[1] How can the library in Snowflake, Arizona (population 3,679) compete with giant megoliths like Time-Warner, the Bells, ViaCom, MCI, Microsoft, Paramount Pictures, and AT&T?

As you explore this book, two things will become apparent:

- There are tremendous opportunities, available to librarians willing to take advantage of them.
- With an understanding of change and how it affects us and armed with clear planning tools, fear and concern can be converted to clear, nonthreatening opportunities to provide improved information service to patrons.

Making the Most of New Technology is divided into seven chapters. Chapter 1 reviews the history of library automation in order to provide a perspective for the future use of technology in libraries. It then looks at the changes automation has brought to libraries, how staff and users reacted to those changes, and how these changes enabled libraries to provide better services. Taking the fear out of change is outlined in Chapter 2. Chapter 3 gives information on factors that affect technological planning. Libraries need to take certain steps before beginning to write a technology plan. Chapter 4 covers those steps and offers guidance and practical tips for carrying out those steps. It also looks in-depth at staff considerations and building factors that need to be reviewed if a technology plan is to be implemented in the particular library setting. Techno-convergence and its role in the library is explored in Chapter 5. This chapter also introduces blended libraries; libraries where technology is blended seamlessly into the library's mission, facilities, staffing, and operations. Blended libraries can be:

- a place to introduce the community to new technology;
- an Internet connection;
- a teaching center; and/or
- a cultural center.

A look at the technology plan itself can be found in Chapter 6, which also presents a template for designing an individual plan and then gives an example of a completed plan. Chapter 7 looks at the future of technology and its relationship to librarians.

Making the Most of New Technology will enable readers to write a technology plan, understand the decision-making process as it applies to technology selection, view technology as a positive challenge, understand how to sort through "technobabble" and identify the wide range of opportunities that exists for improving information services with the new technology. As technology continues to change these services, the librarian must be able to cope with the changes to better serve the patron.

NOTE

1. Kirkpatrick, David. "As the Internet Sizzles; Online Service Battle for Stakes." Fortune (May 1, 1995): 86.

1 LIBRARY AUTOMATION HISTORY AND THE CHANGES AUTOMATION CREATED

To understand where libraries are in their use of technology, we need to understand why and how they began utilizing that technology. This chapter briefly explains that evolution. Who could have foreseen in Michael Faraday's time that electricity eventually would release women to join the workforce; transform the shape of the family; or allow for the building of cities such as Hong Kong or Manhattan, whose skyscrapers could never have been built without the elevator? The introduction of automation in libraries parallels the beginning use of automation in most other areas of business. Automation development is divided into three main stages.

1. Automate what you did yesterday.
2. After automation, what you do changes.
3. Automation causes some transformation.

STAGE ONE: AUTOMATE WHAT YOU DID YESTERDAY

In the 1940s the basic machines available in libraries were manual typewriters, telephones, and photostat machines. Some academic libraries had primitive microcard readers. Catalog cards often were handwritten. People who wanted to reproduce information out of books or magazines for their own use had to copy in longhand what they wanted in order to take the information out of the library. Each library had its own many-drawered card catalog with information about one item on each card. Some entries required multiple cards, and the drawers quickly filled as each library, regardless of type, tried to acquire as much material as possible. Ownership was the guiding principle of collection development. The only way for patrons to have access to information was if it was contained on the shelves of their local public, school, or academic library.

During these years, libraries became seriously overcrowded as the rush continued to jam as much information into each library as possible. Communities, school boards, and universities built new or expanded existing facilities. The value of a library's collection was measured by its size. The library's availability was limited by the hours the building was open. Libraries were the only public source for backfiles of magazines. Researchers had to travel to the site where the documents they needed were located. A standard part of a doctoral student's budget and time allocation was money to travel to the place that housed his or her required books and papers as well as the travel time to get there. Some libraries would mail whole books that were not rare or valuable. It was only in unique cases, however, that they would mail papers, back issues of journals, newspapers, unique items, or local history materials.

MICROFORMS AND COPIERS: ENABLING TOOLS

Microforms were used in a limited way in some large research libraries shortly after the concept of microform publishing was invented by Eugene Power, the founder of UMI, in the 1930s. Mr. Power played an important part in opening the doors to information beyond the local library's threshold. He was working at a printing company, Edwards Brothers, Inc., in Ann Arbor, Michigan, when he invented the concept of microform publishing. In 1935, in two rented rooms in the back of a funeral parlor, he microfilmed the 26,000 titles in Poland and Redgraves Short-Title Catalogue of Books Printed in England, Scotland, and Ireland (1475–1640). Six libraries contracted with him to purchase the microfilm. At the 1936 spring meeting of the American Library Association, Mr. Power introduced his microfilming endeavor. In 1938, he opened University Microfilms, International with the company mission, "to preserve and make available the intellectual inheritance of the literary past, present and future." From its beginning with a single title, many products became available for academic libraries and businesses.

Microfilmed products allowed libraries to provide access to materials when an individual library otherwise would not have the space to store the hard copies. It is not unusual for a large library to hold a large share of its collection on microform. An example is the University of Wisconsin, which had, in 1995, 3,949,109 volumes with 2,317,657 on microfiche or film. Joseph Fitzsimmons, current chairman of UMI, said, "He, [Gene Power], essentially started the whole business of microform publishing. . . . And to this day, I truly believe that the scholarly community can thank Gene for opening the doors to easy and equal access to important information."[1]

Another milestone occurred in 1948 when UMI began microfilming *The New York Times*. The first newspaper to be available on microfilm, *The New York Times*, was subscribed to by many libraries. This newspaper microfilming project was the beginning of microfilm serials subscriptions. Prior to this, most microfilm was of monographs. In the 1950s microfilm started to be an important technology for all types of library use.

In 1959, Eugene Power helped to develop a photocopier that worked directly from microfilm negatives. His association with the Xerox Corporation was instrumental in forming the merger between UMI and Xerox Corporation in 1962. Also, in 1960 Xerox developed and began to market its Copyflow process. This process was an economical way of reproducing and publishing card catalogs using mechanical reproduction. Twenty-one cards were able to fit on a single page. The produced sheets could then be collated into a book format. University and large public libraries produced book catalogs. Production costs were high and staff time required to collate extensive, but it was still less costly than individual typesetting. With only twenty-one cards to a page, the catalogs were heavy multivolume sets.[2]

The importance of the book catalog movement was that first-time catalogs, other than the expensive, bulky National Union Catalog, were available outside of the owning library's card catalog drawers and beyond the individual library's walls. Catalogs could be in the technical services or public service areas, maybe in multiple locations on several floors. The book catalog could leave the building. Now a viable method existed for groups of libraries to produce a union catalog for all members of a cooperative or system. Each library could have their own, on-site copy of the catalog, something that was previously not possible unless each library produced duplicate sets of their catalog cards and these cards were filed at each location. Although the Copyflow process did speed up book catalog production time and reduce costs, the libraries that had book catalogs only produced them yearly. Often, they were not cumulative, so searching was often a tedious process of looking through a large, cumbersome volume and many supplements.

Advances in photographic printing and other printing technologies continued to drive down the price of book catalog production. This factor allowed for an ever-widening distribution of catalogs and made the work of the researcher easier.

The printing improvements, which reduced book catalog production costs, also led to the first wide-scale distribution of reprints. One example is the *Short Title Catalogue of Music Printed Before 1825 In the Fitzwilliam Museum,* Cambridge. This was a book that was only available as reference at the Cambridge University Library in England. It included detailed information on a valuable collection of brittle, place-bound music and was usable only to those who could travel to Cambridge, England, and obtain permission to use the catalogue for scholarly purposes. The catalogue was reprinted and any library that could afford the $195 price could purchase it and make it widely available to its patrons.

In the mid-60s the Xerox 914 machine revolutionized the use of libraries. Large scale, timely, interlibrary loan service was born during this time. No longer did researchers have to travel to the site for information. It was possible in most cases for the information to come to the researcher. A person could make a copy, take it with him or her, and use it later somewhere other than the library. Libraries became publishers of single copies on demand rather than fortress-like retainers or repositories of information and documents. Books began to flow with fewer restrictions between libraries as collection and use policies began to change.

In addition to the use of xerography in libraries there were two other factors that were important components in a library's ability to automate. The development of the standardized MARC format for bibliographic description and the availability of LC uniform catalog cards both played a significant role in library automation.

FIGURE 1.1 Stacks of cards waiting to be filed were common sights before the advent of Online Public Access Catalogs.

MARC AND OCLC: NEW ROADS

Prior to Henriette Avram, Former Library of Congress Head of Technical Services and key person in the development of the MARC format, there were multiple formats used for bibliographic description. It was with the acceptance of the MARC standardization format that thousands of libraries, instead of producing their own catalog cards, ordered uniform cards through the LC Card Distribution Center.

In 1974, the Ohio College Library Consortium (OCLC) was formed to economize on cataloging costs and to avoid duplicate work. A short twenty-two years ago few libraries or librarians understood then OCLC director Fred Kilgore's vision for global access to information. Prior to 1974, the Ohio College Association was an organization that allowed only college libraries in

Ohio to send to a production center in Columbus cards with LC card numbers punched into them. That information was used to produce a set of customized catalog cards for use at the local college library. By today's standards this process seems elementary and can be replicated by the smallest library with a PC, an optical disk drive, and a printer. But, in 1974, production of customized, uniform catalog cards was extremely difficult to achieve.

Fred Kilgore, first director of OCLC, was not content just to produce customized catalog cards. OCLC went online. It overcame huge obstacles in the processes of selecting a computer, customizing the operating system, and pushing the available technology to its limits. OCLC not only survived, it flourished. Libraries outside of Ohio and other types of libraries within Ohio wanted to take advantage of the services OCLC offered. By-law changes allowed service to libraries outside of the boundaries of the state. Continued OCLC development helped libraries in Ohio, Pennsylvania, the Midwest, and elsewhere to standardized cataloging while beginning to create a national database. According to David Bishop, former director of the University of Illinois Library, "There came a critical time when OCLC was either going to become large enough to serve the entire county or a number of regional nodes or replications of OCLC would have to be created. In the early 1970s the general assumption was that these regional nodes would be the way of the future. There were agreements with NELINET and SOLINET to provide regional node services. Why these nodes or replications never came into being is not entirely clear. It may have been that 1) the technology changed to allow OCLC to grow sufficiently; 2) OCLC saw centralization to its political and economical advantage; 3) networks saw problems in being able to replicate; 4) once people started using OCLC there was no real incentive to change; or 5) probably it was a combination of all of the above. The regional replication process was abandoned and OCLC grew to what it is today."[3]

OCLC's role continued to change, grow and expand. In the late 70s, with storage costs declining, large online union catalogs developed. RLG's RLIN large electronic catalog is one example. Electronic mail capability was added to online systems to further enhance interlibrary loan capabilities. The ready access to electronic ordering and reserve functions improved the ease of interlibrary loans. Online catalogs proliferated among all sizes and types of libraries during the late 1970s and early 1980s.

Retrospective conversion of materials consumed librarians' time and the library's resources. Consortia and cooperative projects flourished in the 70s and stand-alone catalogs became online union catalogs available in many locations, the distance from the central catalog creation unit being of little consequence. Most libraries joined and participated in networks and cooperatives. During this time regional, state and multistate networks were born; for example, SOLINET 1973, AMIGOS 1979, OhioNet 1977, CAPCON 1974, FEDLINK 1977, ILLINET 1976, WILS 1972, NELINET 1979, INCOLSA 1974, MLC 1974, and SUNY 1974.

States such as Wisconsin, Illinois, California, New York, and Texas involved libraries of all types in establishing statewide goals and developing statewide networks. The availability of bibliographic records in standard, machine-readable form was a key to unlocking the door to increased, easy, electronic resource sharing. Each state and region developed at its own pace but by 1980 a large number of libraries had online catalogs.

In 1982, Fred Kilgore met with a group of network library leaders in the Southeast to share his early vision of EPIC. EPIC was envisioned to allow contents searching, table of contents analysis and chapter and index searching. After Mr. Kilgore concisely explained his idea, there were few questions and polite applause. Most participants left the meeting confused about what possible technology realistically could perform these tasks and wondered what possible reason would cause a bibliographic utility (OCLC) to move into the information delivery and/or electronic publishing role. Most librarians saw Mr. Kilgore as a man with a vision but a vision that had nothing to do with their libraries' information delivery methods. In 1982, OCLC terminals were viewed only as catalogers' invaluable tools—not as reference or public service tools.

OTHER TECHNOLOGIES

Several other technologies had impacts on the development of improved library service. These included facsimile and CD-ROM, which are highlighted here.

Facsimile

Facsimile machines were invented in 1898. They were used for transmission of crucial military information in both world wars. Some businesses used them in the 60s and 70s. However, in the 1970s facsimile machines were still very expensive and transmission very slow. The transmission speed averaged five to six minutes per page. In the early 1970s several state libraries tested the Group 1 and 2 fax machines for statewide interlibrary loan delivery service. One ten-page article took at least an hour to transmit since the transmission mode was analog. The Wisconsin

Division of Library Service used LSCA grant money to test facsimile delivery between the state reference and loan library and the busiest requesting libraries. The facsimile machines had to be attended constantly as there were frequent paper jams and technical problems. Inclement weather between sites often caused receipt of copies with large, illegible, black-splotched areas where lightning had interfered with the transmission. Although testing of fax use continued for two years, it was determined that the technology was too slow, too costly, and too time consuming except for emergency transmissions. It was not until digitization, a feature of Group 3 fax machines, that communication time was reduced to one minute per page transmission and fax machines became a viable technology for libraries as well as other businesses. Businesses and libraries did not begin to purchase fax machines in large numbers until after 1983.

The Federal Express Company introduced ZAP Mail in 1982 which combined fax technology with satellite communications. Their sales force tried with little success to sell this concept to the large libraries and businesses which could afford the technology. Omnifax introduced a Group 3 machine at the same time and other companies began rushing to market fax machines during the next year. Few standards existed and communication was still slow but with digitization sub-minute transmission became standard.

ZAP Mail from Federal Express, although a project that consumed large sums in production and development costs, was not a commercial success because it could only fax or "zap" to other Federal Express machines. Since few Federal Express machines were purchased it was a closed, proprietary network. This is an example of a specific application of technology that had the early promise of improving communication but was a closed system. Federal Express' emphasis on proprietariness limited their market so narrowly that within eighteen months the machines were no longer available. Their concept that consumers and libraries would want information more quickly than conventional mail or telegraph was on target, however, their use of a totally closed system limited the equipment's usefulness. Increased adoption of facsimile standards allowed other companies' machines to send to each other faxes regardless of brand name. Currently 94 percent of all libraries own at least one fax machine.

Futurist Paul Saffo, in his 1992 American Library Association keynote speech, "The Electric Pinata," discussed a thirty-year cycle of new technology implementation. The fax was invented in 1898; introduced, used in a limited way for fifty years, and improved significantly by digitization in 1983. In 1996 the fax is a common appliance in widespread use with faxing to and from homes, cars, wirelessly from bathtubs, or directly from a computer to fax machine. Many people think of the fax as a technological development that was introduced very quickly and changed people's lives over a few years. In actuality, it was ninety years between facsimile invention and wide scale public use and acceptance.

CD-ROMs

Along with the continued increased use of online catalogs, databases, and fax machines, in 1983 the audio compact disc (CD) began to be purchased for library collections. During this same period some libraries used twelve-inch laser discs for information which required large amounts of storage. In 1983 Pioneer introduced its home video disc unit for full length movies. Initially, it had fifteen movie discs available. In 1983 few technocrats foresaw the 4 3/4" CD-ROM disc as a storage medium except as a passing technology for libraries that couldn't afford online catalogs or for experimenters who wanted to try the newest technology.

Most early CD-ROM projects were projects that required large amounts of cheap storage such as huge bibliographic data bases. WisCat, MaineCat, and SEFLINK were early large scale CD-ROM projects. Several library companies developed CD-ROM catalog products. Production costs were high and all discs were produced outside of the United States (mainly in Europe because there were no American CD-ROM production plants). Fear of impermanence of the data was a factor in the slow acceptance of optical technology by librarians. Since discs had only been produced for a few years, there was no record of how they might last. Some technologists said they doubted CD disc stored information could stay permanent over a ten-year period. Ever-cautious librarians and library preservationists were skeptical about storing important information on this potentially unstable and untested medium.

In the mid 1980s CD-ROMs were used to create reference and bibliographic tools. Indexing was difficult and the software necessary to improve the indexing was even slower to develop. Large bibliographic products required several discs as well as an equal number of disc drives which required significant hardware investment by the library. WisCat, the statewide Wisconsin union database, required four discs. Each CD-ROM work station was completely stand-alone so timely access became a problem and patrons stood in lines waiting to use the CD-ROMs.

Several technological innovations speeded the development of improved CD-ROMs.
    1.   *Compression and decompression: The ability to compress*

and de-compress information so that more information could be stored on each disc. The WisCat statewide database which contained 1,000,000 records in 1983 and required four discs; in 1993 it contained seven discs to contain 4,000,000 records and 15 million holdings.

2. *Caching : The ability of a CD-ROM to store information in such a way that it allows for simultaneous use.* This development eliminated single use workstations which made CD-ROM use more economical.

3. *U.S. production facilities: Turnaround time was cut in half when it was no longer necessary to mail tapes overseas to produce CD-ROMs.* Costs were also reduced as many firms began mastering and pressing CD-ROM discs and competition helped to lower costs.

4. *Improved indexing techniques: software developments allowed more key word searching and less menu-driven restrictions.* Further developments led to any word indexing capabilities which were not available on many online databases.

5. *Built in CD-ROM drives reduced the necessity to "attach" drives to computers and further reduced costs.* In the early 1990s two additional technological enhancements increased the number of CD-ROM products available and improved their overall ease of use.

6. *Re-compression: A compression technique which significantly increased the amount of data that could be stored on a single disc.* Two hundred page books can be stored on a single CD-ROM disc.

7. *Increased standardization: Allows for some inter-operability—the ability of any CD-ROM to access another CD-ROM using any software.* In the near future standardization will permit any 4 3/4" CD-ROM to be played on any machine similar to current universal fax transmission inter-operability.

In review, microforms, copiers, computers, facsimiles and optical discs have moved us from Stage One of automation—automate what you did yesterday—to Stage Two of automation—after basic automation, what you do changes.

STAGE TWO: AFTER AUTOMATION, WHAT YOU DO CHANGES

Since most libraries in America are in Stage Two of automation, it is important to look at some of the changes that have taken place.

SERVICE, NOT SIZE, DRIVES THE MISSION

The most significant shift in libraries because of technology is that the physical size of an individual library matters less. The size of the library building and the size of the materials collection are no longer of primary significance. What matters is how effectively a library can deliver information from a wide variety of sources to users taking advantage of new technology. As Harvard library director Richard DeGennaro often said in the mid-80s, "Technology is making the library available beyond its walls and the resources beyond its walls available within the library." This statement still is valid but could be amended to read "available wherever the patron needs the information."

Collection development is continually evolving from purchasing to providing access. In line with this changing philosophy, library administrators are rethinking their building use and size requirements. Interlibrary loan has changed from borrowing a book or document which will be used and returned to document delivery which is a one-way process of shipping, mailing, express mailing, faxing, online transferring, or e-mailing the information to the requester with no expectation or need for return of the information.

The rapids of change are frothy around the issue of home delivery of information. Most libraries had rules that insisted patrons come to the library to check out materials, pick up interlibrary loan books and read journals in the library edifice. Although some 1970s books-by-mail programs allowed anyone in a service area to avail themselves of convenient, postal delivery, most books-by-mail programs made the potential users prove they were geographically isolated, homebound or disabled in order to be eligible to participate in the mail service. The understanding was that if someone were within a reasonable driving distance of a library and physically able, that person could and should use the regular library.

Some public libraries in the 70s provided reference service via cable television to everyone in their service area. Responses to these projects were varied. Financial constraints limited most of these projects to people with special needs but it quickly was demonstrated that people liked the convenience of home delivery.

In 1984, a Knight-Ridder online newspaper project in Ft. Lauderdale and Miami tried to provide library-supplied, next day answers to individual reference questions directly on a person's home computer. This project was a predecessor to CompuServe. The Broward County Library Reference Department project staff would check their computer screens for questions and provide answers within two hours unless it was after 9:00 P.M., and then twelve hour service was provided. Most days only two or three questions were received. They were typed onto the requestor's monitor and transmitted to the Broward County Library via modem phone communication.

With an estimated 30 million personal computers in American homes in 1995, the demand for home delivery has exploded. It is estimated that approximately 7 percent of libraries now provide either direct dial service into their bibliographic database or home ready reference online delivery service. When personal Internet access is easily available, inexpensive, and hassle-free, the home delivery demand explosion could have the fallout proportions of a nuclear blast.

The changes brought about from the first two stages of automation combine to transform a library's environment and redefine the way the library performs its mission. These changes have been significant. For example, libraries have moved from handwritten cards to OCLC's service of automatically downloading the record into your database at time of order; from date stamps on the ends of pencils to completely automated and in some cases, self-service circulation; and from searching for information through countless books located in far away corners of the library building to finding diverse, multisource information at one workstation which could be located at the library, a business, or a home.

Some libraries have taken the time to redefine their mission to accommodate the changes. Libraries in the 1970s and 1980s tried to provide everything to everyone and their all-encompassing mission or goal statements reflected this desire. Three examples of this are the Broward County Public Library's goal (Ft. Lauderdale, Florida): "To provide the best quality library service, free, to all the citizens of Broward County" (1980); the Montevallo High School Library (Montevallo, Alabama): "To provide all of the materials to meet the students' needs and the teachers' curriculum needs"; and the Free Library of Philadelphia: "To provide the best materials collection possible to meet the needs of the people of Philadelphia" (1979).

As libraries changed their focus from merely gathering and storing information to providing many other kinds of services, professional standards became more service oriented. The Public Library Association moved away from empirical resource standards (i.e., number of books, circulation, and patrons) to output measures (i.e., library use, materials availability, reference, and programming measures). This new view of public libraries and related measures is contained in PLA's *Planning and Role Setting for Public Libraries* (second edition, 1987) and *Output Measures for Public Libraries* (second edition, 1987). Other professional organizations like the American Association of School Librarians followed suit. Its *Information Power : Guidelines for School Library Media Programs* (1988) reflects a similar philosophy.

Libraries of all types reexamined what they did or said they could do vs. what they were doing and what they could do well. The Free Library of Philadelphia redefined its mission from providing everything to focusing on four main areas of emphasis (or "roles" in PLA's nomenclature).

1. Every learner's library
2. Answer place
3. Popular materials center
4. Open a big door for little readers—preschool activities

Fred D'Ignazio defined the school library like this—"the library has to go beyond its technical role of 'Book Center' or 'Media Center' and see itself instead as a 'Human Connections Center'." This view represented a major leap from the vision expressed in 1960 AASL Standards for School Library Programs, which stated "Included in the standards for school library programs will be an expanded treatment in the use of audiovisual materials."[4]

As opposed to Montevallo High School Library's 1980 statement, its new mission statement says that it "seeks to prepare students to enter the world of technology while fostering the concept of the life-long learning by providing current, in-depth information services."

THE LIBRARY'S NEW OPERATING ENVIRONMENT

As libraries are evolving, the environment around libraries is changing. The role of some cooperatives is changing. Early cooperatives were developed to take advantage of new technology, shared resources and to distribute cost factors. In response to intense financial pressure, some cooperatives are becoming competitors. As competitiveness increases it is increasingly difficult to trust and maintain the commitment to shared projects and databases. As mass data storage costs continue to drop dramatically, sometimes it is easier and cheaper for individual libraries to own resources they previously would not have had the storage capacity to afford. The CD-ROM version of the Oxford English Dictionary takes up one disc and costs only $895. The printed form is twenty volumes, weighs 137 pounds, and costs $2,700.

The impulse to return to independence and autonomy is strong for some smaller libraries which felt forced or coerced into cooperatives because they could not afford what their patrons demanded. Cooperatives appeared to be the only way to meet these needs. Some libraries see that the purchase of information on demand, commercial access agreements, and cheap optical reference products combine to make the original reasons for cooperation not as important as the advantages of autonomy.

Another change in the library environment is the erosion of the "free" library ethic. Almost simultaneous to the introduction of photocopier use in libraries, librarians saw technology as a revenue generating source. It was argued that if people wanted free access, they had it either by remaining in the library to read what reference materials they needed or by laborious free hand copying. Copying was seen as a convenient and time-saving devise and not as a way of providing primary use. Students in every age group were happy to pay the small charge to be able to take the information away with them. Because people were willing to pay, library policy setters argued it was okay to charge for convenience in the same way that public libraries charged for best seller use and postcard notification of reserves. Over a period of many years, general acceptance of photocopying charges led to the introduction of the philosophy that it is justifiable and acceptable to charge fees for any information that is delivered by a machine; i.e., online data bases, microform printouts, CD-ROM printouts, and fax copies. Ironically, information that flows out of a librarian's mouth is still free.

As vast amounts of information became available cheaply to entrepreneurs and information brokers, competition increased between private information companies and libraries. At that same time, many large public and academic research libraries started charging fees for in-depth reference services. It became harder to provide all services for free.

In Great Britain in 1988 a *Green Paper* was issued by the government, which madly pursued any revenue generating scheme. This paper defined free service so narrowly that charges were proposed for any reference inquiry beyond directional questions and a charge for every entry into the library was even suggested. This paper's plan was not accepted, but several of the revenue generating suggestions were implemented.

With the increased chance of profit from information of all

kinds, information delivery is becoming viable from all types of commercial sources which would have been judged unlikely information providers two or three years ago. Major motion picture producers, cable television franchise owners, telephone companies, and video game producers are all desperately vying for a piece of the commercial information market. Delivery of information rarely has been such a hot, front page issue. As associate dean of New York University Libraries, Nancy Kranich states in *Library Journal*, "The convergence of new communications technologies and deregulation through several recent court decisions has blurred the more traditional lines between information carriers and providers. As a result, the jockeying among telecommunications, cable, and entertainment/retailing companies over who will control the technomarket-place's conduit and content is already intensifying."[5]

APPROACHING STAGE THREE: AUTOMATION CAUSES SOME TRANSFORMATION

The challenge facing libraries in the next decade is not the decision whether or not to implement new technology or the decision concerning what machines to purchase and when to purchase them. The challenge is to implement new library cultures and management structures in our somewhat ailing industrial age libraries.

What lessons learned from libraries' brief technological past can guide us through the inevitable transformation? Where are Zap Mail and Knight Ridder On Line today? Did they get lost in the unbreakable miasma of proprietary systems, products, and machines that could not work or link with others? A key word which will be increasingly important in our technology future is *interoperability*. The ability to access any machine using any software.

As standardization of equipment and software compatibility increases, as cross platforms are improved for use of products regardless of equipment or operating systems, interoperability has become and will increasingly become an achievable goal. OCLC's WebZ introduced in June 1995, has the potential of bringing the electronic library to every user's desktop via the software and databases libraries already have. WebZ is a seamless gateway from the World Wide Web to local information and is one more example of what interoperability can achieve.

Electronic delivery of full-text, full-image information regardless of a user's location will be an increasing patron demand. Books by mail, fax to home, and dial access will be an extended continuum moving toward a wide range of wireless personal access. The focus for libraries will continue to be on access to information rather than on ownership of information. This concept will be further detailed when we discuss the "virtual" library in Chapter 3.

As commercialization of information and availability of recreational "reading" of slick, flashy, multimedia packages bombard the current library users, all types of libraries need to improve user interfaces. Don't make the interfaces just user-friendly, but also user-cordial. A joke appeared in a national magazine depicting those who could not learn to navigate the Internet as the roadkill on the information highway. A continuing role of libraries is easing access to all types of information. As commercial products proliferate, comparisons will be made between a product a person has tried at the electronic boutique and what he or she has used at the library. Seamless interfaces which provide instant information presented in a user's native language in large type with auditory options (such as multilingual capabilities) and a pleasing display are required if libraries are to continue to compete with commercial products. Are you beginning to feel technostress? Are these questions becoming overwhelming?

How do you provide this improved, user cordial service with an eroding tax base and increased competition for public dollars? You already work overtime, and are worn out from trying to improve service. Some of you and your patrons are content with the status quo. You just bought a new computer last week and that means you don't have to change anything for a long time. Learning to recognize change, including the shifting expectations of patrons, can provide a strong basis for understanding the opportunities available through change.

NOTES

1. "Farewell to Eugene Power: The Father of Micropublishing." Serials Perspective, UMI Ann Arbor, Vol II, No. 1 (Spring-Summer 1994):3.
2. *"Farewell to Eugene Power,"* pp. 3–4.
3. "History of Networking in the Southeast," Speech of David Bishop (Oct. 17, 1986) Southeastern Library Association Meeting, Atlanta, GA.
4. D'Ignazio, Fred. "How to Contain an Ever-Expanding Job." *School Library Journal* (January 1995):33.
5. "The Selling of Cyberspace : Can Libraries Protect Public Access?" *Library Journal* (Nov. 15, 1993):35.

2 TAKING THE FEAR OUT OF CHANGE

Change: so much has been written about it by so many that there doesn't seem to be a lot left to say. This chapter will focus on the "how" of change—specific methods you can use for dealing with it effectively. Sometimes change will be something you create; sometimes it will be imposed on you. You will learn to enjoy being an agent of change. You will not be the only one affected. Staff members, patrons, board members, elected officials, vendors—almost everyone who has anything to do with your library—will feel the effects of change sooner or later. You can fulfill your role as an agent of change in a way that makes change exciting, positive, and energizing or it can be deadly, negative, and enervating. Choose to make change healthy and useful. The ideas in this chapter will help you do that.

UNDERSTANDING AND DEALING WITH CHANGE YOURSELF

WHAT IS CHANGE?

Longshoreman-philosopher Eric Hoffer said, "A revolutionary movement is a conspicuous instrument of change."[1] Technology in the library business certainly qualifies as a revolution. As mass movements, revolutions create vast, and usually, irreversible changes. These changes are lasting and ongoing, not cyclical. They affect the very core and structure of library work. New technology is not a passing fancy like mood rings, snap bracelets, and eight-track tapes. It is not a fad that will briefly appear on the horizon and then fade away to be replaced by another short-lived phenomenon. It is changing the very basics of the profession and will have long-term effects.

What is change and what makes it seem mostly negative? Change occurs when something new, different, or unusual is requested, required, or demanded. A new, different, or unusual product, service, method, practice, way of thinking, whatever the change may be, disrupts the familiar and comfortable routines. If it is an imposed change, one that you are "forced" to make, in a sense you're being told that your "old way" is no longer acceptable. Something you have done successfully in the past is now wrong; it must be abolished, supplemented, or replaced with something that to you is alien, foreign, unknown, untried, or untested. Chances are you might feel resistant to changing even when a change might be a positive one. Perhaps you face a change that is not imposed on you, but is something you want to create. You may have an idea, solution, decision, or more effective way to do something. You will have to get others to accept the change and try to minimize their resistance to it.

WHY DO SO MANY PEOPLE RESIST CHANGE?

As you look at each of the following reasons why people resist change, examine them from two points of view. First, if the change is being imposed on you, which of the following items could you use to replace your own resistance with better understanding of the reason for change? Second, what things can you do, stop doing, or do differently in each case to minimize the resistance someone might have to the change you need or want them to make?

One of the primary reasons people don't like change could be because they may not have been involved in some way in creating the change. Even if the creator of the change means well, to some degree people usually feel defensive about a change which is imposed without their participation. Remember "taxation without representation"? It's the same idea. "Change without consultation." Barriers and obstacles, sometimes even hostilities, arise when change is imposed without involvement by those affected.

Change usually requires new or different knowledge, skills, or attributes from those affected by it. People resist change when they are afraid they will fail in implementing or carrying out the new scheme of things. This fear of looking bad, appearing to lack the experience or ability to deal with a new product, service, or technology is a paramount reason for people to resist change. No one likes to fail. An inordinate fear of failure is a strong motivation to fend off or try to defer or delay any change.

Another negative perception of change is that it probably will cause more work. People often see a change as an *addition* to their workloads, rather than as a *better*, *smarter*, *faster*, *easier* way to do their jobs. If someone looks at change as a frightening event which will add to their already heavy workload, that change will be resisted.

Some people resist change because it doesn't seem like a good investment of time or money. "I can do it the old way a lot faster than trying to learn the new way" is a common resistance statement. So is "Why spend all that money when the way we've been doing it works OK?" If people don't understand the time and cost benefits of a change, they will resist it.

We all get accustomed to doing our jobs in ways that are familiar, comfortable, sometimes almost rote. Change disrupts our cultivated patterns of work. Upheaval, contradiction, unlearning, and relearning can all be viewed as negative elements of change. These elements shake our confidence and bring turmoil to our customary way of doing things. So, we resist. It's natural. Before the change, people know the routine so well they often don't have to think to do some parts of their jobs. When changes come, each new step requires thinking and rethinking.

Take a moment right now to cross your arms over your chest. Sit this way for just a minute. Now cross them again, but opposite the way you had them before. If your left arm was on top of your right, put your right on top of your left. Confusing? Difficult? Does it feel odd or uncomfortable? You'll feel better if you put your arms back in their original and familiar position. Try it. What do you think? A permanent or structural change, like new technology, doesn't allow going back to the old way (like using file cards in a wooden card catalog). There is likely to be some resistance to change when it involves casting aside the way things always have been done. Change can bring another kind of disruption. It can break up or create new personal relationships, job teams, or work groups. A lot of people will resist a change that might require disbanding or restructuring a long-term working relationship.

Suppose a change is imposed and people wonder, "What will happen if we don't do it?" Further imagine they, in fact, don't implement the change and nothing significant happens. Conversely, imagine that change is imposed and people ask "What will happen if we do it?" They do make the change and still nothing significant happens to them. What have they learned in these cases? The consequences of the changes are meaningless. If nothing bad happens when they don't change and nothing good happens when they do, they will be apathetic. It doesn't matter to anyone else, so why should it matter to them?

Another reason why people resist change is that they imagine it might detract from the satisfaction they get from doing their jobs in the way they already know. Perhaps a library employee particularly enjoys personal contact with patrons. It may be very rewarding to offer help, guidance, and assistance through personal service. Along comes technology in all its wonderful electronic, computerized, CD-ROM, PAC, DVD and other initialed acronymic outfits. Suddenly, there's a machine providing self-service to the patron and staff-patron contact is diminished. How does the employee find job satisfaction? Anticipating these possible consequences of technological change, the employee who always enjoyed working directly with library patrons probably will be resistant to change. The "old way" preserves job satisfaction.

The six predominant reasons people resist change are concern about:

- Non-involvement
- Added work
- Cost and/or turmoil
- Lack of commitment
- Loss of job satisfaction

Now let's look at the wide variety of ways in which people actually resist change.

HOW PEOPLE RESIST CHANGE

We're all familiar with open rebellion, mass uprising, revolutions, and other forms of obvious resistance to change. Strikes, job actions, so-called "Blue Flu" and other blatant acts, including violence and sabotage, are wide-open forms of resistance to change. There are many other forms which are less dramatic, but no less serious indicators of resistance.

A change may cause some people to argue, grumble, or complain much more than usual. They might spend a lot of time hankering for the old way of doing something. You'll hear phrases like, "We've never done that before," or "That'll never work," or "What's wrong with the way we used to do it?" Finding fault is a spin-off of this way of showing resistance to change.

When a change is put in place, some people will show how they feel by asking continually for directions, procedures, or answers, very often to the same questions. They repeatedly ask about nit-picking issues as a way of demonstrating their displeasure or reluctance to the change.

Equipment, tools, instruments, supplies, or materials connected with a change will break down, not work, be missing, or run out much more frequently when the change isn't seen as good or favorable. This is another example of how people resist a change they don't fully understand or in which they weren't involved.

Avoidance behavior is yet another classic symptom of resistance. If someone doesn't like a change, a way to avoid it is to be absent or consistently late. You may see excessive sick leave being used or people leaving work early or taking longer breaks or lunch times. Often this is a subtle way of showing resistance to change— by avoiding it.

HOW TO MINIMIZE YOUR OWN RESISTANCE TO CHANGE

Many people get mired in certainty and stability. They think, plan, and operate as if nothing is going to change. They have no mechanism for dealing with change. When change occurs, they are lost. They view change as an exception rather than part of daily life. Not only is change bound to happen, but also now it's dynamic and frequent. It's coming faster and in larger chunks than ever before. You must be prepared to make adjustments rapidly. You have to be able to accept change for yourself before you can become an agent of change with others. Imagine that you are the one asked to implement a decision or new way of operating. Imagine further that you're not sure it's the right way to go or the best way to do it. You have some unanswered questions, some reservations. You may even feel a little resistance to arbitrarily installing this change that has been imposed on you. What can you do?

There are five general questions you can ask of the person or board who wants you to create change. Asking upward in the chain of command will help clarify the change, and perhaps reveal aspects of the change of which you weren't aware previously. If you have some reticence about the change, get answers to these open-ended questions:

1. How can I better understand the reason for the change? Do we agree on the cause and need for change?
2. How can I be involved in creating the change? In what way may I participate in the change?
3. What will be gained by changing? What are the benefits?
4. What will not be lost if we change? What assurances can we give?
5. What will be lost if we fail to change? What are the negative consequences of not changing?

Work through the answers to these key questions before trying to implement a change to which you are not 100 percent committed. It will make your task relatively simple if you run into resistance from others. If you're not fully convinced the change is beneficial, others around you will sense that and may drag their heels. Your own lack of commitment may make your job more difficult. Consider the opposite situation: you may not like the change; others around you do. Finding that you are the "misfit" is an undesirable discovery. Get yourself in sync with the change. Understand it. Get "fired up" about it. You'll find that implementing an imposed change can be more pleasant than you might think.

WHAT IF THE CHANGE WOULD CREATE AN UNTENABLE OR FRUSTRATING SITUATION?

Let's suppose for a moment that a change is to be made. You know from all of your experience that it probably will not work at all or, at least, not the way the change-imposers think it will. You find yourself frustrated, at a stalemate, not content to push through something in which you don't believe. You have four options in this situation:

1. *"Fight" to change the situation to make it better.* Be creative in devising different ways to deal with the problem. Consider alternatives. Exercise some options. Then, put on your "sales hat" to persuade and enable the decision-makers to buy your alternative ideas.

   If you have exhausted all your sources and resources for trying creatively to change the untenable situation, move to Step Two.

2. *Accept the situation as it is, but without complaining.* As long as you are doing something constructive to create a positive outcome to the frustrating situation (Step One), you are allowed to complain or grumble a little bit. The moment you move to Step Two and consciously decide to accept the situation as it is, you must give up your griping rights. No whining. No grousing. You have chosen to stop fighting for change. You have opted to "love the unlovely." Live with it and get on to bigger and better things.

3. If you will not accept the situation which is so frustrating to you or you will not accept without complaining (out loud or internally—both ways are apparent), then you need to *remove yourself from the situation you find so unpleasant.* Get a new job. Update your resumé. Deselect yourself. Remove yourself from the scene that you are unable or unwilling to fight to change, that you will not accept as is, or that you will not accept without complaining. Prepare to go to Step Four, if you do not exercise Step Three.

4. The first three steps are positive and reflect individual courage and strength. Step Four is negative, self-defeating, and the sure sign of a loser. Step four is *deteriorate*. If people do not choose one of the other three ways of dealing with a frustrating situation, then by default they are choosing to deteriorate. They will stay in the situation, but not fight to improve or make it better. They will not accept it as it is, but will gripe and complain. They will stay in the position or organization, creating unpleasantness for others and for themselves. They eventually become "maliciously obedient." They do whatever they are told, even if they know it's wrong. People who select deterioration, instead of the other three choices, usually mark an end to their own personal and professional growth.

Be smart; be effective; be professional. Don't opt for Step Four. Go back and review the first three choices and reevaluate if they are possible and positive. You can be an effective agent for change even when the situation initially seems totally frustrating, angering, or unacceptable.

HOW DO YOU GET OTHERS TO EMBRACE CHANGE?

You have an idea, the solution to a problem, a suggestion, a decision—a change that you believe in and that you need others to accept. No matter how good that change may be, it will not work if others don't understand, accept, and implement it.

You know how people resist change and why they resist. Carefully think through and answer all the questions on the "Idea Analysis" sheet. If the change you propose is truly a good and necessary one, you will get the support, endorsement, and adoption your idea deserves.

FIGURE 2.1 Idea Analysis Worksheet

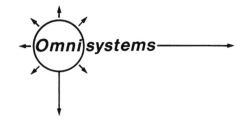

IDEA ANALYSIS

In trying to create constructive change, there is always a chance someone will resist that change. Analyze your ideas thoroughly by answering all of these questions; you will greatly minimize resistance to change.

1. My idea (decision, solution, suggestion): _____

2. Who I have to sell it to:_____ Others directly affected: _____

3. Here is specifically <u>why</u> this change is needed: _____

4. How sure am I that the listener <u>understands</u> the <u>reason</u> for this change? _____

5. Do we agree: there is a problem? _____ on the cause of the problem? _____

6. How can I get the listener <u>involved</u> in this change? _____

7. What does my idea cost? $_____ Time _____

8. What does my idea save? $_____ Time _____

9. What else can be saved? Space? Tools? Equipment? Overtime? Confusion? Policies? Image? People? Paperwork? Facilities? Other problems? _____

10. What will the listener <u>gain</u> by changing? (Benefits) _____

11. What will the listener <u>not lose</u> by changing? (Assurances) _____

12. What might the listener <u>lose</u> by not changing? (Negative Consequences) _____

13. How does my idea contribute to other objectives? _____

14. What objections could the listener possibly have? _____

15. How can I offset each of these? _____

16. What is the best <u>method</u> of presenting my idea? _____ Who can I try it on? _____

17. How can I improve or clarify the description of my idea? _____

18. How can I dramatize it? _____ What audio-visuals can I use? _____

19. What is the best time, timing, and place to present it? _____

20. What similar idea has ever been presented and rejected? _____ Why? _____

21. What benefits does my idea have that offset the reasons for prior denial? _____

22. Additional benefits, features, techniques, and methods that will reduce possible resistance to my idea:

    _____

23. Checklist for mental and physical preparation of presentation: _____

24. To whom I will present my idea: _____ Time and date: _____ Where: _____

25. Additional notes: _____

    _____

    _____

Here are some comments and amplifications of the items on the sheet. Feel free to make copies of the form to use with each change or idea you want to implement.

1. Be very specific in your description of the change.
2. Identify the key decision-maker or approver. Don't overlook others who will have an impact.
3. Be precise.
4. Get valid feedback. Ask open-ended questions, not "yes" or "no" questions, to assure complete understanding.
5. Your idea should close the gap between what is happening and what should be happening with regard to any problem. Do you know what needs to be done to close the gap? Do you know how to do it? Are you allowed to? Are you capable (physically, academically) of doing it? Do you really want to do it?
6. Remember: Emotional involvement is more important than intellectual involvement.
7. Be specific. Consider all budgetary items. Measure time in large chunks (hours, days, weeks).
8. Be specific. Point out all savings. Measure time saved in smaller increments (minutes, hours, days, percents of total time).
9. Brainstorm here. Consider and list all probable, specific savings to aid in selling your idea for change. Get input from others.
10. List all the benefits to those affected by your idea for change. Consider the impact of it on the person, the team, the organization, patrons, boards, faculty, friends of the library, partners, commissioners, staff, outside groups, and any and all others.
11. This element often is overlooked, but is critically important. List all the major items that will not be lost or negatively affected by your idea for change. You need to offer assurance and proof that your idea will not cause those touched by the proposed change to lose things they value. Remember that people value authority, seniority, office location, equipment, title, hours of work, and pay benefits. These are all items of concern that you might be tempted to take for granted or think someone else would realize without having them pointed out.
12. Try not to make this a threat, but rather an explanation of what might happen if we fail to change.
13. List, as many as possible, other departmental or organizational goals which will be influenced favorably through the acceptance of your idea for change.

14. Write down everything that possibly could be used to toss cold water on your idea. This will be a huge help to you in planning and making your presentation.

15. Have at least two ideas for dealing with each possible objection.

16. What's your strong suit? Do you do best with audio-visuals? Computer Screens? Models? Speaking using a large chart or overhead projector? Working from prepared overhead charts or creating your own on the spot? Having a Question-and-Answer format? Handouts? Printed reference materials? A formal written proposal? Find a few people who know nothing about your idea. If you can explain it well enough that they understand and endorse it, you're ready to polish it up for presentation to the decision makers.

17. Make your own presentation so clear that a twelve-year-old could understand it. Streamline! Big-time decision-makers have short attention spans.

18. Drama, emotion, pizzazz, and warmth always sell better than presenting only cold, hard impersonal facts. People learn more by seeing than by any other way. Use visual aids.

19. Timing is critical. A great idea given at the wrong time or place can do more harm than good. PLAN, PLAN, PLAN.

20. Don't repeat someone else's past mistakes. Make your change significant.

21. Account for changes that have occurred or you have created since a similar idea may have been presented.

22. Have all of these readily available in your mind and notes in case they're needed.

23. Be rested, fresh, and ready to go. Prepare a checklist to make sure you have everything you need. People don't buy ideas for change when the presenter forgets to be fully prepared.

24. The action line: Do it!

25. This is especially important for listing follow-up notes after your presentation, which is valuable information for your next change.

If you thoroughly review the Idea Analysis Worksheet, the chances of getting your idea for change accepted and implemented are greatly increased. Idea creators are a dime a dozen. Those who can sell their ideas are priceless.

Observe constantly that all things take place by change, and accustom thyself to consider that the nature of the Universe loves nothing so much as to change the things which are, and to make new things like them.
—Marcus Aurelius Antoninus

FIGURES 2.2 and 2.3 Both books and computers constantly change.

CHANGING EXPECTATIONS OF PATRONS

After you have:

1) analyzed your style of implementing change;
2) decided why you want to change; and

3) established the plan to make the change; before you move ahead, stop to consider
4) the changing expectations of the people you serve.

The average American's ability to have quick access to information has changed dramatically with several improvements in technology. One of these improvements is the advent of reasonably priced, mobile cellular phone service. As the cost of the phone service continues to decrease dramatically and the reception range begins to increase, more people will use this technology to help provide wireless access to quick information. Most airlines have phone access built into the back of the airline seats. New mobile phone PDAs (personal data assistants) include a component that allows the owner to fax information from the cellular unit.

The use of overnight or express mail services is another commonly accepted method of providing quick access to information. Personal fax machines that operate cheaply through home phone lines are one of the fastest selling home electronic devices.

Up until several years ago, library patrons were satisfied with interlibrary loan materials that took an average of six to eight weeks to obtain. Patrons waited because they were accustomed to waiting for other things such as out-of-stock parts for car repair, merchandise that had to be sent from an out-of-state store or items ordered through catalogs. Today, most commercial firms use some type of overnight coast-to-coast delivery or global delivery. All types of delivery have become faster.

Library patrons who receive their first fax answer no longer are considerate when staff tell them that most information takes several days to a week to arrive. The expectation of receiving information quickly is not just a big city expectation. Federal Express advertises "We go to the ends of the earth to deliver quickly." Americans can dial 1-800-FLOWERS from New York City (population 8,546,846) or Sunflower, Mississippi (population 729) and have flowers delivered the same day. With commercial service improving so dramatically, it is reasonable to expect information to be delivered quickly within and from another library information center.

Telephones are easy to use. Televisions are easy to use. Commercial vendors are designing information products including traditional library delivered information sources using phones and televisions.

Unless libraries provide easy-to-use access, commercial information vendors will continue to increase their share of the information delivery market. The methods and tools to improve ease of use are available to libraries.

What are features that make some commercial products successful?

1. Easy to use instructions with a maximum of one or two steps.
2. Use of natural language.
3. The ability to type a sentence or word grouping without having to know search thesaurus terms is an advantage for some products.

Compare these two ways of finding information and think about which you would prefer:

FIGURE 2.4   Traditional Online Catalog/Catalog Using Artificial Intelligence

OLAF	INFOFIND
Welcome to OLAF	Welcome to Infofind
There are three modes to search the catalog. Novice Intermediate Expert	What would you like to find in the catalog?

Press F1 = Novice
        F2 = Intermediate
        F3 = Expert
	I would like to find books about canals

Press F4 = Title
        F5 = Subject
        F6 = Author
	32 items found
	Canals in America
	Canals in Florida

F5 = Subject Canals	[Artificial intelligence employed to select canal and book as what the person most likely wants]
Not on file	
Help—The word you have selected is not a subject heading see thesaurus for headings	
F5=Subject Aqueducts	

The OLAF Catalog required seven steps just to locate the subject heading for the patron's request whereas Infofind delivered appropriate citations with only three steps. The Infofind search engine employed natural language; OLAF was menu-driven. Also contributing to Infofind's quicker delivery was the fact that its design indexes every word whereas OLAF's design uses a restricted thesaurus like the Library of Congress Subject Headings.

Compare the following two keyboards:

FIGURE 2.5 Catalog Using Natural Language

Screen 1

Sample Catalog

1. Books Only

2. Magazine Articles Only

3. Books & Magazine Articles

MOVE BAR TO SELECTION With (↑) (↓)KEYS AND PRESS ENTER OR ENTER FUNCTION NUMBER

Screen 2

WHAT WOULD YOU LIKE TO FIND IN THE CATALOG?

TYPE IN WHAT YOU NEED TO FIND

Typically, commercial products use fewer keys and give fewer choices than most library-developed products. They also have color coding to improve ease of use and feature easy-to-understand commands. Other commercial product keyboards use the words "yes" and "no" for responses rather than symbols to mean yes and no. Again, this change is to improve the ease of use. Some products use touch sensitive screens. One example of this is Kid's Catalog. Kid's Catalog was first developed by CARL, a library company that grew out of the Colorado Alliance of Research Libraries. This clear picture recognition catalog combines pictures, simple commands, a touch screen and eye-grabbing clear color to introduce children to the use of an online catalog. The product jointly produced with the Denver Public Library has been so enthusiastically received that CARL is selling the Kid's Catalog as a separate product that can be added to non-CARL catalogs. Pam Sandlian, Children's Library Manager of the Denver Public Library, conceived the idea of Kid's Catalog. Its design goal was to make the library an easier place to use. "The library is a complicated place. Kid's Catalog is a way to uncomplicate it for children."[2] An adult version, Everyone's Catalog is now available for adults.

Besides fast delivery of information, another expectation that is changing is the patron's desire to leave the library with the actual information rather than just finding citations to information that can be obtained at a later date.

When the old, reliable, green *Readers' Guide to Periodical Literature* was the main source to finding the location of information, patrons were satisfied just to find a citation. When periodical holdings were loaded into and included in automated public catalogs, they could find a citation more quickly and without browsing through multiple volumes and supplements. The patron, citations clutched in hand, would then attack the collection, hoping the book or journal would be on the shelf intact, not mutilated or misshelved. Information Access Company's (IAC) Infotrack and similar periodical products short-cut the search procedure by having the citation include a location number for the role of microfilm. Roll microfiche was another advancement in the quest to improve ease of finding information. The searcher pressed a button to quickly search through the alphabetic sequence.

With the development of full-text, online services, multimedia products on the World Wide Web, and full-text CD-ROM products, patrons' expectations changed drastically. Citations alone were no longer enough. Full-text availability at one workstation became the norm. Libraries of all types are working toward patron access workstations that will provide information just as

ATM machines now dispense money, rather than just give information about an account balance. Library patrons using home computers expect not only to obtain information easily in full-text but also to have it available directly from their home/work-place/car. In 1983, when CD-ROMs were introduced for information storage, all of the library products contained bibliographic citations. In 1992, of the 518 most popular databases, forty-two were full-text. Many products, both optical and online, are becoming not just full-text but full-image. Full-image means the text, along with images, graphs, and charts, are all available to be viewed in their entirety and be printed.

With technology changing so quickly, we all experience difficulty keeping up. There are 1,000 books published every day in the world. The number of people using the Internet all over the world increases daily. One of the gurus of Internet Publishing, Brewster Kahle, President of WAIS, says in summarizing the changes taking place that the Internet Consumers credo focuses on:

Relevant: What I want
Easy: How I want it
Fast: When I want it[3]

Another statement concerning meeting patrons' expectations in an ever-changing world is the goal of the Los Alamos National Laboratory Research Library's *Library Without Walls* Initative: "The creation of a network of knowledge systems and machines which facilitates synergy and collaboration between people."[4] It is paramount to keep the needs of the library's customers/clientele always in the forefront of the planning effort.

Have users changed their style of usage? According to a 1993 study of fifty university students by Judy Anderson at Arizona State University, Tempe, "A balance of on-line help products and staff interaction is needed when providing help for users....that even with exposure to more advanced searching techniques, patrons still rely on simple subject searching."[5]

Changes in the technology that facilitate information provision as well as declining costs of storing and providing information allow librarians and information providers unique opportunities to meet the changing expectations of patrons.

NOTES

1. Hoffer, Eric. *The True Believer*. New York: Harper & Row, 1951:13
2. Pam Sandlian, Personal Interview, Nov. 1, 1995.
3. Lunin, Lois. "Where are the Internet Consumers? Just follow their eyeballs." *Information Today*: 1995 33.
4. Luce, Richard E. "Shaping the Library of the Future: Digital Developments at the Los Alamos National Laboratory's Research Library." From a conference paper presented at InfoTech '94, Oak Ridge, Tennessee, October 24-25, 1994, p. 2.
5. Anderson, Judy. "Have users changed their style? A survey of CD-ROM vs. OPAC product usage." *RQ* No. 3 (Spring 1995):362.

3 FACTORS THAT AFFECT TECHNOLOGICAL PLANNING

This chapter explores seven major factors that affect technological planning. These seven factors are:

1. Coming of age in the Nintendo Generation
2. Portability of Information (Old Books vs. New Books)
3. The Fate of Books in a Time of Virtual Reality
4. Technology's Downward Reach
5. Fiber Optics
6. Changes in Mass Storage
7. Phone-Costing Changes.

Each of these seven areas will be explored for its effect on planning for library technology. This chapter is not a basic planning guide for managing change. For that information refer to *Managing Change: A How-To-Do-It Manual for Planning, Implementing and Evaluating Changes in Libraries* by Susan C. Curzon (1989) and *Strategic Planning* by M.E.L. Jacobs (1990), which are part of the Neal-Schuman "How-To-Do-It" series. Those two books will provide step-by-step guides for basic planning. This chapter nudges you to look ahead and peek into the twenty-first century. If you begin to feel technostress as you read this chapter, review Chapter Two again before you continue.

FACTOR 1: COMING OF AGE IN THE NINTENDO GENERATION

During a recent presentation to a fifth grade class demonstrating a PDA (Personal Data Assistant) and a small hand-held electronic encyclopedia, I explained that workstations and Gameboy-sized computers had replaced the card catalog. A hand shot up and the eager fifth grader asked, "What's the card catalog?"

Although not all school libraries or small libraries are automated, it is the rare child who comes into a library today that hasn't played on a Gameboy, or Nintendo home entertainment system for several years. In a recent survey of 10,000 computer owners done by Computer Intelligence-InforCorp, 71 percent said they use their computers most often for entertainment.[1]

A news report in *School Library Journal* discussed a *Wall Street Journal* report that even though computer buyers say they purchased their personal computer to figure out their home finances and/or to improve their children's homework, they actually used them most to play games or chat.[2]

CDI Television systems and some reference home products have joy stick controls and right to left thumb controls similar to commercial video game controls because most children know how to use these two features easily. If you hand an adult a palm-sized computer, he/she usually supports it with one hand and presses the key board with the other. Hand a child a small computer and they will grab it like a Gameboy—both hands partially supporting it so both thumbs are on top for the controls.

FIGURES 3.1a & 3.1b Adults hold hand-held devices differently than children.

Nintendo-age children, besides having double-jointed thumbs from hours and years of playing video games, expect fast action and clear, colorful video game–type screen display. For example, the Kid's Catalog, produced by CARL Company, has many of the elements of video game interactivity and is thus an innovative example of a library product specifically designed for this generation.

"Video" children read video game magazines to learn how to improve their video game scores. There are many game magazine titles including GamePro, Sega, Visions, Electronic Gaming Monthly, Video Gaming Monthly, S.W.A.T. Pro, and the Game Players Encyclopedia. These magazines, which average $5.00 to $10.00 apiece, give previews and reviews of new games, tips of how to play better, information about new technology, and developments. Tiny 1" x 1/2" code books, Game Genie, and other video game enhancers give clues and teach methods to add infinite lives to video persona for kids who pay $15.00 apiece for the game enhancers. Video arcade games are a multimillion dollar industry. Would children and/or their parents pay $5.00 to $10.00 for a key or code to discover information for a term paper or book report? Yet, many parents pay to subscribe to information products in order to enhance their child's chance to improve school success. Video game producers, as a way of encouraging parents with the idea that some video games are educational, are including information bits on the game CDs. One example is on the Sega Genesis CD game Ecco the Dolphin. If you move to an emerald on the game screen, you get information facts about the life and habits of bottlenose dolphins. Then you return to the action game across the seas, under the polar caps, to the lost city of Atlantis, back 55 million years in time. Video games and information are blending to create new products that increase commercial success.

Nintendo-age children like small containers for information and recreational games. For many years they have carried, in small cases or in their hands, their game cards, Gameboys or pocket arcades. Although some adults are frustrated by the miniature keyboards found on hand-held devices (PDAs), by the time the Nintendo generation comes of age, they will be comfortable with small devices that resemble and feel like the portable video game units they grew up with but that do much more. For example, a recently marketed PDA weighs only eleven ounces and measures 3 1/2" by 7", yet allows the consumer to wirelessly send and receive e-mail, faxes, access online services and exchange information from personal computers. It has pen input, a keyboard, and an intuitive touch screen. Except for the keyboard, it looks very similar to a hand-held video game.

The Nintendo generation children experience changes in other areas of their lives that potentially change how they approach the information seeking process. Emphasis on global education is expanding children's view of their world from their local city, town, village, state, and country to the entire world. Changes in the past five years in enhanced school curriculum, the addition of more inclusive textbooks, and the emphasis on multiculturalism and languages all provide expanded points-of-reference for students. The concept of hopping on a global information highway is not alien or unfamiliar to young people. Children would be comfortable with president and CEO of OCLC Dr. K. Wayne Smith's description of OCLC as "a global resource, a global asset, a library commons for the world."[3] Children have read for several years about virtual reality projects not only in the gaming and computer magazines but in *Weekly Reader* and *Scholastic Magazine*. For children who spend many hours per week playing video games, have school classrooms with computers, and play at home with computers, a large amount of their daily life is spent imaging themselves somewhere else and interacting with imaginary video characters.

Virtual reality is an easy next step. These kids will hang out at coffee house cafés such as the Cybarian in London. This café offers coffee and snacks as well as places at the table to plug in a laptop and check e-mail. Another café in Atlanta even provides the computers so all you need is your Internet password, and a credit card to get information and snacks.

Nintendo introduced Virtual Boy with a $20 million marketing campaign and hoped it will attract the Nintendo generation to cheap virtual reality. According to Nintendo President, Hiroshi Yamauchi, "Virtual Boy...transports players to a 'Virtual Utopia' with sights and sounds unlike anything they've ever experienced—all at the price of a current home video game system." The Virtual Boy hardware has two components: the HMD and double-handed controller. The HMD bolts to a metal stand (Virtual Boy is designed to be played seated at a table) and you press your face into its foam rubber eye cups to play. The stereoscopic display utilizes tilted mirrors and is a licensed version of Reflection Technology's Scanned Linear Array display and provides a field of view of 360 degrees that is monochrome (red). The spatial resolution is approximately 380 x 220 pixels of four bit grayscale and is amazingly sharp. The single color displays seem to make the image very easy to converge. Nintendo has added interpupillary distance and pixit pupil adjustment controls, making this one of the sharpest views seen in an HMD at any price point.[4]

FACTOR 2: PORTABILITY OF INFORMATION: INFORMATION ON THE GO

In the 1950s and '60s information was place bound. Before the advent of copy machines people had to travel to the place where the information was located to use it. Traveling to the location of the information is no longer necessary. Cheap mass storage and lower cost hardware provided the capability for the information to be at whatever location the individual chose. With the global reach and lightning speed of the Internet, it will play a major role in the transformation of libraries. For basic information on the Internet, refer to *American Libraries'* "Internet Librarian" columnist Karen G. Schneider's *The Internet Access Cookbook* (Neal-Schuman, 1995). This easy-to-read introduction to the Internet is particularly helpful to librarians in small and medium-sized libraries.

An encyclopedia is one example of an expensive, multivolume reference book that now can be carried by middle income individuals in a briefcase, purse, or back pack. The portable, wireless information packaged encyclopedia can be accessed anyplace, anytime, and leaves several bookshelves empty. As the box of information on page 42 about the evolution of the encyclopedia shows, information is no longer locked up in the library. An individual can now access information that was once contained in multivolume expensive encyclopedia sets only found in libraries from his or her home, office, or even from a mountainpeak.

Another example of information on the go is the Physician's Medline, a highly-demanded, but costly, medical reference tool. Now it is available on a CD-ROM disc with 200 full-text magazines indexed in the *New England Journal of Medicine* on each disc, updated quarterly, and yet it costs only $399. The disc can be carried easily and popped into a doctor's or hospital's computer workstation for quick referral to the most current medical information. If you were to stack one year's worth of journals indexed by Medline next to the 555-foot-high Washington Monument, the stacked journals would be 800 feet tall, almost one-and-a-half times the height of the Monument. It would take 960 CD-ROMs to store that same information. Those 960 CD-ROMs, if stacked on top of each other, would only be about thirteen feet tall!

CD-ROM products are increasing daily. In 1994 there were over 6,000 CD-ROMs in print. Thirteen percent of home computers in 1995 had CD-ROM drives.[5] Many of these CD-ROMs

FIGURE 3.2 The evolution of general encyclopedias both parallels and demonstrates the increasing portability of information.

1910	The Book of Knowledge
1917	First edition of the World Book—eight volumes —Costly, only owned by rich —Very difficult to revise—took years —Held by libraries in single copy, reference
1930	Encyclopedias increasingly popular — Sold door-to-door
1935	Large one-volume-like Columbia Encyclopedia — Sold on the installation plan — Most were general knowledge encyclopedias — As printing and paper costs dropped, so did the prices of sets of encyclopedias
1950	Improvements in Xerography
1966	Prices drop again — New Book of Knowledge printed
1971	World Book grows to twenty-two volumes — Many libraries provided circulating copies — More specialized encyclopedias available
1986	Electronic encyclopedia—CD version of Academic American Encyclopedia
1990	Compton's first CD-ROM encyclopedia — 1 Disc—$395 cost — Indexing superior—easy to use — Colored images, sound, charts — Easy to revise
1991	Many other CD-ROM encyclopedias — Improved indexing improved easy-to-use ability
1991	Encyclopedias available on tape to load into individual library's reference database — Available online in homes and businesses
1992	Costs drop dramatically — CD-ROM encyclopedia $99.00 — Checked out as circulating CD-ROM in libraries — Promoted for home use — Included "free" on many new computer workstation packages
1993	Personal Data Assistants include encyclopedia feature in the basic unit at no extra cost
1994	Several PCs include CD encyclopedia as part of basic home computer package
1995	CD encyclopedia included as one of six discs in reference package for $29.99 — Some encyclopedias available over the Internet

fit into small portable units. Some library staff still view CD-ROMs as a passing technology and argue over how many years CD-ROMs will last, and continue not to purchase CD-ROMs. The CD audio market in the early 1980s drove the production of cheap CD-ROMs. In the early 1980s libraries were one of the few industries storing information on CD-ROMs. Several times a commercial technology giant such as Sony tried to promote and sell CD-ROMs commercially but were not able to build a sustaining customer base and withdrew their early commercial products.

In the early 1980s all CD-ROMs were pressed outside of the United States, mainly in Europe. This added to their cost. Early indexing was not user-friendly. As CD-ROM production facilities began in America, as indexing improved and compression techniques allowed more information per disc, more commercial discs were introduced. All standard-sized computers sold in the United States now contain a built-in CD-drive. This is surely indicative of a technology that's here to stay.

Each six-month period sees the introduction of a new or improved personal data assistant. The first PDA (Personal Data Assistant) produced in the United States had some difficulty recognizing handwriting, but the encoding mechanisms improve constantly. Voice recognition is a feature included in some small computers. As pen and voice recognition features improve in commercially-available products, library patrons will demand that similar technology be available to them at or through the library.

FACTOR 3: THE FATE OF BOOKS IN A TIME OF VIRTUAL REALITY ("OLD" BOOKS VERSUS "NEW" BOOKS)

I, too, said I would "never" curl up with a computer in bed. Some people might prefer machines, but not me. Books are comfortable, convenient, easy-to-use, good-feeling, hand-fitting, familiar packages of information and recreation. They can be easily carried, pulled out, and sampled everywhere and anywhere.

At a conference on new technology the keynote speaker, attired in pajamas, rolled a bed onto center stage, reached beyond the podium, grabbed something and curled comfortably in bed. After the audience had recovered from its surprise, he pulled out his tiny hand-held powerbook and proceeded to read an expanded book. He held it up on its side and over his head and all the other comfortable familiar positions we "bed readers" assume with a book. Only after all these machinations did he turn to the audience and speak. "See, it is just as easy to curl up with a computer." He certainly made his point.

In the past, the major drawbacks to continued, non-eye-straining, easy reading of a computer screen have been flicker, poor contrast and color, and poor quality resolution. Many of the palm size computers are now flicker-free. Apple's Power Book is an example of a flicker-free screen. The contrast of a good quality book is 120:1. The contrast in most pre-1993 computer screens was 50:1. The contrast in notebook computers is 100:1 and improving with each new version. High quality color is a standard feature of most notebook computers and coming soon to PDAs. Resolution is the area where books still out-match laptop computers. The newer screens on high end workstations with 250 dots per inch rival paper and ink but most smaller units are at paperback book resolution. Within a few years laptops also will have resolution at the same level as paper and ink.

WHAT IS AN EXPANDED BOOK?

An expanded book is an example of a blended technology. An expanded book looks like a book. It is read on a screen but it retains its page-to-page approach. As you finish reading one page and indicate that, the page rolls over just like with a regular paper book. The computer book retains the functionality of a paper book. You can turn down pages, underline sections, make notes in the margin, and put paper clips on pages for easy return. It is amusing to watch the corner of a computer screen appear to turn down or a tiny "paper" clip appear when you signal it. However, in addition to these paper book features, the expanded book has auxiliary features that expand the boundaries of a book. The expanded book can include not only text but also the original source material. The source material may include the text of a play in a "book" of criticism or whole speeches. An expanded book contains all five elements of interactivity: audio, text, video, graphics, and animation.

There are three basic types of expanded books:

    1)   "Electronic" book,
    2)   Data Games, and
    3)   Interactive Literature: Intertainment.[6]

Most electronic books originate from electronic files produced by word processors that then generate printed copy. The file remains an electronic version of the original. Much like the first print books, the early electronic books have come under criticism as being less inviting than their print versions.

Most electronic games follow a basic storyline which creates a fantasy world or simulates reality but are structurally similar to books. Most electronic information packages contain a game. Data games use richer graphics and sound effects which make them more entertaining. Some games do permit interactivity by the user, but the interactivity is limited to storyline and movement. There are few data games that have an interactive storyline that changes according to the game players' actions.

Interactive literature was created by the entertainment industry. Joining the computer to other machines such as videodisc and videotape players lets the reader (player) not only watch the information (action) but also interact with what is happening. When the "intertainment" source includes virtual reality the "reading" mixes the real with computer graphics. Films, novels, and plays attempt to create an involving artificial experience, but with virtual reality added the participant is engulfed in the story being told and can change the outcome.

An example used by Norman Desmarais is "a reader could begin in the 'real world' as a modern-day Alice and enter into virtual Wonderland. Here, she would meet the various characters—who would appear as her real-life friends and acquaintances—and then participate in several adventures, depending on the choices she makes. She could even experience different adventures if she returns to the same location more than once."[7]

All of these types of electronic books will play a part in information providing. The electronic books will change definition and direction as the technologies emerge and mature further. David Macaulay, in an interview with *School Library Journal* about the making of the CD-ROM product from his book *The Way Things Work*, talks about the CD as a "translation." He discusses the possible problems of the entertaining methods used to present the information overwhelming the information itself. He urges producers of CDs to make a good match with the medium and the content when they convert existing books to CD, and that they should realize that all books are not convertible.[8]

CD-ROM products can also spawn related books as is the case with *Myst*, the popular CD-ROM game. *Myst* topped the CD-ROM best seller lists for many months. To capitalize on this popularity, the game's creators wrote a book called *Myst: The Book of Atrus* which was a prequel to the events included in the original game.

One example of an expanded book is one that covers a

Shakespeare play. In the expanded book one would have the text just as you would in the paper book. At the touch of a key, the text could appear in modern English or old English. One could hear the voices of famous Shakespearean actors reading the parts as the words were highlighted on the screen. One could view the video of the play or a section of the play. Another feature of this particular expanded book is that the reader could choose to read the lines of the characters in the play and an actor would fill in the rest of the lines contrapuntally. Other expanded books have musical or historical themes. When the text explains the development of the telegraph, the reader could hear the first message clicking across the wires, see a picture of the inventor, or hear him talking in his own words about the invention and how it came to be. With all this information, visual images, and sound contained in one package, it's easy to see why that package is called an "expanded" book.

Many students who entered schools of library and information science from the 1970s to the 1990s did so because of their love for books. Did we ask them what books? Whether they are hand-tooled leather covered rare books, paperback books, reference books, expanded books, or comic books, as a concept, all books represent a contextual format for a package containing information or recreation. Does the Nintendo generation, their television grandparents, and video parents care about the format of the packages? Should leather, hand-tooled, artistically beautiful covers be provided for Personal Data Assistants and lap or palm computers? Radio Shack currently sells a leather slip case for their Personal Data Assistant which provides the tactile feel of a regular book. Motorola gives away a leather carrying case with its Envoy and Marcus wireless communicators. Accept the reality of this change and treasure the opportunities it provides to better serve the community's information and recreational needs.

VIRTUAL IMAGING

One step beyond the expanded book is virtual reality, an outgrowth of video games which evolved from the pin ball machines that captured children's imaginations—watching the silver ball spin, dip, and take alternate paths. The dinging sound, flashing lights, and vivid color all combined to create a challenging, action-packed game. Video game action takes place on a screen rather than the horizontal pin ball track. Video games provide more interactivity. Up, down, right, and left were the four choices for movement in early games. Joy sticks were added to provide more precise movement in later versions. In order to keep competitive, video game features proliferated and revenues soared.

Free standing arcades and huge video arcades furnished youth with a gathering place to challenge the screen villains.

The ongoing popularity of video games encouraged creators and producers to continue to augment the games. As digitization has enhanced the color features of television, the same features have been carried over to the video game market. Screens which once appeared flat have become three-dimensional and holographic. The game player often is surrounded by the game capsule. The child sits down in a chair that is part of the video game apparatus. When you step into the game and insert a token into the slot, the sound and action surround you. It is only a short step from these wrap around games into virtual reality.

What Is Virtual Reality?

Virtual reality reflects a television picture to the eye so the picture appears to be floating in space. This reflection is the virtual image. There are three components necessary to project a virtual image.

1) A miniature video display system located within glasses that fit around your head or is contained in a stand into which you look.
2) A belt pack containing a miniature television tuner, a battery, and an interface system. In some versions, this is miniaturized and built into the glasses. It also can be in a freestanding unit as in Virtual Boy. The unit resembles a set of large binoculars on a tripod.
3) An interface mechanism that connects the first two elements to a VCR, camcorder, and a cable television. The fast changing technology of virtual reality does not always require this connection. It depends on the specific application.

The natural progression for Nintendo age children who have video games available on their television, portable games for traveling, as well as coin-fed machines in arcades, grocery stores, airports, gas stations, and convenience stores, is virtual reality centers and virtual amusement parks.

In 1994, a store called Virtual World opened in a trendy youth oriented shopping center in Chicago. The staff teaches customers how to use the technology and what to expect from the experience. A virtual reality session is twenty minutes in the session and five minutes in interpreting the results. Most of their customers are young adults. Virtual World centers are a creation of Tim Disney. Mr. Disney is planning a major virtual amusement park to capitalize on the imaging technology. If such imaging technology is available with instructional sessions in shopping centers, won't consumers also expect to find similar information technology in libraries?

FACTOR 4: TECHNOLOGY'S DOWNWARD REACH

Other factors that affect technological planning are wide range technologies that are available in the home to library users. What causes technology to become increasingly home-based?

THE DRAMATIC PRICE DECREASE IN EQUIPMENT

In 1987, when the Adonis Project began to store full-text health and science journal information on CD-ROM, the project required a CD-ROM jukebox worth more than $230,000 to retrieve information. Subscriptions to this prototype document delivery service cost about $40,000. The jukebox held up to 200 discs and contained the information from about 220 periodicals. Today a person can go to his or her local department store and purchase a 100 CD disc changer for under $1000. The Sony Disc Changer machine is billed in many advertisements as serving as "a library and the librarian, your entire CD collection remains in mint condition inside this dust resistant changer, constantly "on-call" for instant play." Although this particular machine only works with audio disc, there are jukeboxes that hold up to 328 CD-ROMs, the price is under $25,000 and falling rapidly.

For most consumer electronics, equipment price drops of 50 percent in the first year are not unusual. Most of the CDI units for television were introduced at $999 and now are under $400. Sales of these units have been disappointing and several companies have withdrawn their early product entries.

NCs, or network computers, are no-frills computers that perform only basic computer functions. They cost only $500. Rather than use computers for number crunching as in the past, with the daily growing connections to the Internet and the digital web that links about 50 million computers worldwide, a growing number of people use their computers as communication devices. Larry Ellison, Chairman of Oracle, the world's second-biggest software company, is betting that future PC buyers will select a machine that has the functions people use the most: word-processing, e-

FIGURE 3.3   A CD-ROM Jukebox. Reproduced with permission of Todd Enterprises, Inc.

mail, Internet access, and video conferencing.

There are other technology giants who question whether consumers will buy a basic unit with only the power of a 486 PC. To keep to the $500 price, many popular PC features would have to be dropped; for example, a color monitor, CD-ROM drive, and both floppy and hard drives. The new unit would look much like a laptop with a keyboard, monochrome flat-panel screen, a modem, and a mouse. It would be powered with a superfast chip. Nathan Myhrvold, chief of advanced technology at Microsoft, is very skeptical about a stripped-down computer. "People want more from their computers, not less."[9] In direct opposition is noted futurist Paul Saffo, at the Institute for the Future in Palo Alto, California. He emphatically states: "The PC is dead. It's the horse and carriage of the Information Revolution."[10]

AVAILABILITY OF THE INTERNET TO CHILDREN

With Pacific Bell providing free access to the Internet for all public schools and public libraries in California, this is but one example of an increasingly large number of children who have access to the Internet. The ability to access resources for class projects will never be the same. Instead of being limited to the books and resources from their school and local public libraries, children can use resources from all over the world. One example of expanded access is the school access project in California, where the connection from a California school allows students to study moon photographs from the Clementine satellite, watch a laser sear a concrete block at Lawrence Livermore National Laboratory, and access research papers on gene cloning from the University of Chicago. All of this is free over the Internet and does not require leaving the school grounds. There are those that say learning how to navigate the Internet is as important to a student as learning to drive a car. North Carolina and other states are currently planning statewide access to the Internet. Canada's national government has funded Internet access to over 5,000 schools throughout Canada.

CHANGES IN THE WORKFORCE

The U.S. Bureau of Labor Statistics reports that over 2 million good jobs vanished from the U.S. economy between 1981 and 1992.[11] The Bureau also projects long term job loss nationwide in food processing, apparel manufacturing, pharmaceuticals, publishing, and trucking. There are also dramatic declines in bank teller and secretarial jobs. As global competition increases job security will be more uncertain. These changes are occurring, according to Ron Miller, past President and CEO of Washington Library Network, WLN, " . . . because technology allows the advanced world economies to produce more with fewer people at a lower cost, and unskilled as well as highly skilled jobs are exported to other less expensive world-wide labor markets eager for our business."[12]

FACTOR 5: FIBER OPTICS

The expanded capabilities of a fiber optic cable provide almost unlimited telecommunications power for a library. With dial-in access, libraries can be available twenty-four hours a day, seven days a week, with connections around the world. A single fiber optic cable—thinner than a single strand of hair—can simultaneously handle 30,000 digital phone calls. It would take forty copper cables, each four inches in diameter, and $13^{1}/_{3}$ feet of cabling to handle the same 30,000 calls as one hair slender fiber optic cable. The cabling plan for a new building is one of the most important parts of a new building plan. If there is not enough space to run additional cabling through as the services in a library grow, service has to be curtailed or costly conduit added. Fiber optic cable consumes only 1/160th the space of a copper cable. In most telecommunication companies, maintenance accounts for 25 percent of company costs. The maintenance costs of a fiber optic network are about one-fifth those of a wired network.

Talk with your area phone provider to find out if fiber optic lines are available in your city or area. Most telephone companies install fiber optic cables as they are needed to replace old copper cable. Large cities have the highest priority for the installation of fiber optic lines.When there is a natural disaster that destroys cable, it is replaced with fiber optic. Many cities along the Mississippi that suffered devastation from flooding now have fiber optic lines. Installation of these lines is very costly so rural areas have the lowest priority for replacement. In order to take advantage of the increased capabilities of fiber optic lines, both the receiver and the sender must be using fiber optic lines. In some areas of the United States, cable television stations are installing fiber optic cable. They realize the necessity of remaining competitive by providing additional channels. In the same way as more phone calls can travel over a fiber optic cable so can addition cable television signals.

FACTOR 6: CHANGES IN MASS INFORMATION STORAGE

Cheap mass storage mechanisms also affect technological planning. Cost of optical storage and online disc storage both have dropped significantly.

ONLINE STORAGE

In the past only the largest academic, public, and special libraries could afford the storage costs associated with locally mounting large databases. When serials and journals began to be available online, few libraries could afford the storage space cost to take advantage of having the journal information available from each workstation rather that just a few designated workstations. Currently small- and medium-sized libraries are able to consider tapeloading reference materials and full text magazines on their local databases. All sizes of libraries, including the smallest, are able to benefit from cheap mass storage.

WHAT ARE SOME OF THE TYPES OF OPTICAL STORAGE AND HOW WILL THEY BENEFIT MY PATRONS?

CD-ROM

CD-ROM stands for compact disc-read only memory. A CD-ROM is a silvery 12" or 4 3/4" circular plate that is encoded with information. There are several methods of encoding that are only important if you plan to create your own discs. Most discs are created by stamping the information into pits on the CD-ROM. One 4 3/4" disc can store 700 million characters of data, or 2,000 floppy discs or 240,000 sheets of paper, the equivalent of the text of six sets of encyclopedias. As computer designers develop new methods of decompressing and recompressing the data on the CD-ROM disc and double dipping the disc they hold even more data. Unlike traditional print media, where subject or index words are used to find information, the software used with CD-ROMs allow every word to be searched, which in turn leads to more successful searches. CD-ROMs are used to store bibliographic information as well as journal and a wide variety of other reference materials. More technical information on CD-ROMs can be found on pages 90–91.

Video CD

Video CD standards are still emerging. In most products, the medium allows for seventy-two minutes of video on a single disc; audio quality is superior to that of other mediums. Vendors are working hard to provide the most color enhanced video CD. Most vendors use a product name. They all hope that their product name will be the name by which video CD is called. Some on the market now are CDI (Compact Disc Interactive), CD32, and 3DO. This technology is a blend of television and personal computers. It puts the power of a personal computer into your television. This probably will be a short-lived technology as DVD (discussed in the next section) will probably achieve market dominance.

Digital Video Discs

Plan to see a great push for DVDs beginning in 1996. Digital video discs are five inches in diameter, so CD-ROM players cannot utilize them at this time. There are many people in the entertainment industry who are certain that DVD will revolutionize the convenience and economy of home video entertainment. These discs can store up to twenty times as much information as existing CDs and CD-ROMs. They will require a new player to accommodate their size, however. Some experts predict that videotape will soon be obsolete when DVD achieves prominence in the market. The discs will not require the high maintenance of video tape. But before you rush out and purchase a DVD player, remember that some sages also predict that you will dial up everything you want to watch on your television information appliance. Optical technologies are still in a transitional phase. As with most new technologies, prices will drop quickly if the product captures the consumer market.

Rewritable Optical Disc

There are two types of rewritable optical discs, phase-change and magneto-optical. Two major PC makers plan to equip servers with a 46B removable magneto-optical (MO) drive instead of a hard disc in order to reduce hard disc failure. Optical discs' key selling point is removability. If a drive crashes, you can remove the disc and recover your data on another drive. Optical discs are more stable than magnetic hard discs because there is no contact between the head and the disc. Standards are just being finalized for new optical discs. Continue to watch this medium in the future as optical discs could be a major contender for mass desktop storage.

Optical Storage Technologies on the High-Density Horizon

Although none of these technologies are available yet, I mention them here so you can watch for further developments as these technologies emerge. All three could have profound effects on mass storage.

1. *Blue laser technology.* CD-ROM drives currently use red lasers. Blue lasers increase the potential for data storage because they can read a narrower track on the disc.
2. *Cholesteric liquid crystal (CLC).* This solution explores the possibility of adding additional layers of data to the conventional CD-ROM design. Reveo Company has tested a six-layer prototype with almost 25GB capacity! This would dramatically increase storage capacity.
3. *High-density read-only memory (HD-ROM).* This storage method uses a focused ion beam micromil to store materials by colliding atoms in the ion beam. The data can be written on one-inch steel pins that hold 180 times the readable stored data of a typical CD-ROM at just a half percent of the cost. This claim was made by the

technology's developer, Los Alamos National Laboratory Physical Chemist Bruce Lamartine. The data pins could remain stable for 5,000 years because they are non-flammable, non-malleable, and don't react to chemicals.[13]

THE SEVEN ADVANTAGES OF OPTICAL STORAGE

As you begin your technological planning, remember the seven advantages of optical storage and weigh them against other technologies as you progress. As product features change and are expanded, these seven factors could be used as a measure with new technologies.

1. Ease of Budgeting

Although some progress has been made in standardizing and limiting online costs, purchasing an optical product outright allows you to know the initial costs and the multiple user costs for the whole year upfront. Using optical storage helps the library to gain control of the open-ended cost associated with providing access to computer readable information. The motivation for using optical storage need not be lowering costs, although that would be advantageous, but the goal should be controlling costs. This medium allows you the ability to set a fixed budget at the beginning of the year and meet patrons' ever-increasing demands without exceeding the yearly budget. As the number of CD-ROM titles has increased the cost per title has been reduced also. In 1987 the average price per title was $1,273. In 1994 the average price was $510. Many commercial reference products are in the $19 to $49 range. The CD-ROM player base has grown from only 9,000 in 1986 to well over 7,000,000 in 1994. The CD-ROM titles available have grown from 0 in 1980 to 1,400 in 1991 to 5,700 in 1994.[14]

2. Easily Maintained Product

Unless optical products are networked, they depend only on electricity. In those cases there are no telecommunication lines to worry about—only electrical lines.

3. Minimal Staff Training

Search out products that are easiest to use and buy those that have the most patron self-service features and require the least amount of staff training. The PC environment makes a superior interface possible. All levels of staff should be able to use the equipment. Natural language, word grouping ability, relational databases, and ever-expanding index points increase the number of successful searches and reduce the amount of staff training.

4. Increased Patron Self-Service

New products include more prompts and expanded help screens. They allow patrons to browse the shelves electronically and to get readers' advisory information. Each product enhancement includes additional features that make technology easier to use.

5. Expanded Access at Reduced Costs

Denser storage equals lower costs. Libraries, regardless of size, are able to provide more information for less money than they were in the past.

6. Strong Patron and Staff Acceptance

Technological products are changing from user-friendly to user-cordial. Consider the patron who needed to look up thirty business addresses in phone books. He or she would have to search through bulky, cumbersome telephone books, know the proper search terms, and hope to find the information if the page hadn't been torn out. The same search can yield more current data and can be done much more quickly using a CD-ROM.

7. Combination of Text, Audio, and Video

The expanded power of new media allows not only full-text but full-image to be displayed. Full-text is just words while full-image includes words as well as pictures, charts, graphs, and other graphics. Full-motion video is now also available with some of the newer products.

HOW WILL THE INTERNET AND WORLD WIDE WEB BENEFIT PATRONS?

In the 1960s the Department of Defense created the Internet to link military installations, government laboratories, and contractors. That interconnected network (hence the term Internet) was decentralized to the point that it operated without a central authority or computer so that it could remain operable even in the event of a nuclear attack. By establishing open systems standards that allow computers all over the world to relay messages and transmit files, the Internet has sparked communications innovation on a global scale. Open first only to academic institutions (including academic libraries), with increased commercialization, all types of libraries can now establish a presence on and use the Internet, either free-of-charge through statewide arrangements, or through commercial services for a fee.

The World Wide Web (WWW) is currently the trendiest part of the Internet. The WWW opens up cyberspace to anyone who wants to publish information or set up a virtual shop. That it promises a direct link to consumers is what makes it so commercially popular. A Web site consists of a computer hooked up to the Internet and loaded with software that allows it to receive and answer queries from users. Web traffic incorporates full-color graphics, music, and video. Following a standard set of rules for presenting data, text, images, videoclips, and digital information, Web sites can link information from any point on the Web to any other point. Movement from Web site to Web site is seamless. The Web uses an array of innovative, user-friendly graphical interfaces (GUIs—pronounced goo-ies) including Cello, Mosaic, Netscape, Hot Java, and others. In January, 1995, 20 percent of libraries reported using the World Wide Web.[15]

OCLC's WWW home page is so popular that in a three-month period (September to December 1994) more than 15,000 sites all over the world accessed almost 100,000 files through it. Twenty percent of that traffic was from Asia and Europe. OCLC's home page includes samples of electronic journals, news releases, research reports, online technical bulletins, product information sheets, white papers, and annual reports. Their address is: http://www.oclc.org/

What are the advantages of providing Internet/WWW access to patrons?

1. The Net and the Web are available twenty-four hours a day. Unlike most libraries, they are never closed. If a patron wants to use the Internet at 3:00 a.m. and the library provides dial-in access, the patron can.

2. The available resources are truly global. If you participate in reference Listservs such as STUMPERS, the answer to your question is just as likely to come from Australia as it is from the next closest library.

3. The Internet's value cannot be matched by hard-copy materials. While no library is large enough nor rich enough to buy and store all of the Internet's resources in a single site, connect charges to all the Net's resources are miniscule.

4. There is amazing patron awareness of the Internet. Many people connect to it in their work environments. Print, radio, and television media have flooded everyone, everywhere with hype about the promise of this technology.

5. The Web's exceptional color graphics and seamless interface make it a user-cordial product. The difficulty is not in getting people to use it but rather in getting them to stop so that the next person waiting to use it can.

FACTOR 7: PHONE-COSTING CHANGES

Continual technological change is driving down many of the elements that make up the cost of a phone call. Transmitting a call from New York to London now actually consumes the same costs as transmitting a call from one house to its next door neighbor. It is believed that phone companies may soon begin to change their long-distance pricing structure from the length of the call to a flat subscription rate. If this occurs, most ordinary conversations will cost nothing extra, regardless of duration or distance:

> The demise of distance as the key to the cost of communicating may well provide the most significant economic force shaping the next half-century. . . . Revolutionary as the change in pricing will be, its impact will be magnified by two other earth-moving changes. One is the high increase in capacity and the portability of the telephone.[16]

All new technologies go through many refinements before their full potential can be realized. The telephone is not a new technology. What is new, however, is the effect that almost costless communication will have on two other common pieces of equipment. As the transmission of information increasingly is digitized, the previously existing boundaries among the telephone, the television, and the computer will continue to blur. Combine these three types of equipment and all new kinds of products and services can evolve from the brain and memory of the computer, the entertainment and fun of television, and the two-way human interaction of the telephone.

For libraries as well as big business and government, this telecommunications revolution will be unsettling. It will put more power onto the desks and into the homes of ordinary people. Customers and voters will find it easier to make comparisons, get information, cross borders, and bypass society's traditional gatekeepers. Libraries will need to continue to explore new roles and respond to new patron demands.

What will it be like to live in a world where it costs little more to talk to a friend or colleague on a different continent than to your next door neighbor? What will happen when communications costs come down to next to nothing which is likely to happen in the early part of the twenty-first century? These transformations will alter decisions about where people live and work as well as traditional perceptions of national borders. Any activity that relies on a screen or a telephone can be carried out anywhere in the world. Educational institutions and companies will change the way they do business. For the old and the isolated, cheap communications will greatly enhance lives: if a phone costs nothing but the base subscription fee, homebound people can use the line all day long at no additional cost. It is difficult to predict the future of a new technology and guess at its impact, but it is nonetheless possible to be alert to changes as they happen and to explore the potential on our work and our lives.

Technology should not be embraced just because it is new and might have widely-touted features. Each technology must be carefully weighed for its potential value to improve service to patrons whether from within the walls of the library or from remote locations. According to the late John Swan, of Bennington College Vermont Library, "If we are to have any hope for assuring the quality of information and achieving real equity in its distribution in this brave new world, we must conform the reality that the new technology affects the way people understand the information it carries. It affects the very nature and scope of their inquiry—once again the medium is the message.

"The universal tendency among the patrons of our electronic tools is to regard the menu of alternatives offered up on a particular screen as a world sufficient unto itself. If we can't get them to move beyond Infotrac, we respond by connecting their screen to an online public access catalog (OPAC) and a dozen other databases. . . . It is still as true as ever that a screen has essential limitations as a source of information. . . . The human mind is not and cannot be just another perfectly interfaced terminal in the chain of workstations making up the virtual library."[17]

These seven factors affecting technological planning also affect the librarian as libraries embrace technology and evolve.

NOTES

1. "Home computers used mainly for fun and games." *School Library Journal* (January 1995):16

2. "Home computers," *School Library Journal,* p. 16.

3. Smith, K. Wayne. "The Global Community of Research Libraries; Proceedings of the 13th Annual Conference of Research Library Directors," March 13–14, 1995, OCLS p. 5.

4. "Nintendo's New Baby Boy." *VR World* (May/June 1995):14.

5. "Vital Statistics: Home PCs," Cyberscope Section, *Newsweek* (Oct. 9, 1995), n.p.

6. Demarais, Norman. "Models of the Electronic Book," *CD-ROM Professional,* (May 1995):113–114.

7. Demarais, "Models," p. 114.

8. Olson, Renee. "The Way Things Ought to Work." *School Library Journal,* (May 1995):23–26.

9. Meyer, Michael. "Is Your PC Too Complex? Get Ready for the 'NC'." *Newsweek* (Nov. 6, 1995):101.

10. Meyer, "Is Your PC Too Complex?", *Newsweek,* p. 101.

11. Miller, Ron. "Work in the 21st Century." WLN Participant March, April 1994 p. 2.

12. Miller, "Work in the 21st Century."

13. "New Optical Storage Technologies on High-Density Horizon," *CD-ROM Professional* (Oct. 1995):16.

14. *CD-ROMs in Print*: Meckler 1994.

15. St. Lifer, Evan. "Catching on to the 'Now' Medium: *LJ*'s Multimedia/Technology Study," *Library Journal* (February 1, 1995):44.

16. "The Revolution Begins At Last," *The Economist* (September 30, 1995):15.

17. Swan, John "The Electronic Straitjacket." *Library Journal* (October 15, 1993):42.

4 WHAT TO DO BEFORE WRITING THE TECHNOLOGY PLAN

Even the best-written technology plan cannot be implemented successfully if the staff is not committed to seeing it put into place. The more you can understand about the people with whom you work and their reactions to new technologies, the better your chances are of developing a plan that will work.

STAFF AND BUILDING CONSIDERATIONS

WHAT WILL HAPPEN TO "MARION THE LIBRARIAN" IN THE TWENTY-FIRST CENTURY?

The typical library and information school student is a white woman with an undergraduate degree in English or History. She is at least thirty years old and often is attending library school as a second career.[1] Her graduate record exam scores are high; according to Dean Barbara B. Moran of the School of Information and Library Science at the University of North Carolina at Chapel Hill, "Given the grade point averages and the graduate record examination scores of persons admitted to our school, I am convinced that they could be admitted into any professional school on campus."[2]

Why do people choose to go to library school? According to a recent article in *Glamour* magazine, librarians are info-surfers. Walk into most libraries today and you'll be hard pressed to find a librarian thumbing through the card catalog. Perhaps more than in any other career, technology has transformed the work of the librarian, leaving her with more time to do what she does best; provide information.

Thanks to training in databases and other computer tools, today's librarian is an information guru who designs systems, evaluates new technologies and coaches people on how to find the best sources online.[3]

A study done in 1989 showed that most people who went to

FIGURE 4.1 Before libraries embraced technology, library staffs spent hundreds if not thousands of hours performing easily automated functions like filing catalog cards.

library school had previous experience in a library and the majority responded that someone had influenced them, often a librarian.[4] This study was conducted seven years ago. Will the previous experience prospective students have changed significantly? As more and more jobs in libraries are automated will fewer students and summer workers be hired? If fewer and fewer young people have experience in libraries, will less of them pursue careers in libraries? As most libraries buy books already processed, don't have cards to file, and don't repair books, what jobs will student workers have? Library staff who are able to combine technological expertise with a librarian's tradition of commitment to serving others will continue to be very much in demand. As more and more advertising about the information highway is aimed at the general public there will continue to be confusion.

Librarians are in a unique position to provide this necessary information. Dr. Laverna Saunders of the University of Nevada uses the term "cybrarian" to describe a professional staff person working in a blended, virtual library.

PLANNING FOR TECHNOLOGY

When you start your planning for new technology, there are ten considerations to keep in mind in preparing and working with your staff. Even if you work in a one-person library, don't skip this section. Most of the concepts are valid regardless of staff size. Ernestine Rose, in 1954, gave an interesting description of the difference between libraries of varying sizes. "I sometimes think that the chief difference between a small library and a large one is that in the latter there is a job for each worker while in the former there is one worker for all the jobs."[5]

1. Include all staff.

Regardless of the size of the library, all staff should be included in the planning process. If you are the only staff person in a public library, include the library board members, friends of the library, and/or volunteers. In a school media setting, incorporate the teachers who are regular library users, a committee of administrators, teachers, students, and also volunteers. Often there is a tendency to include only those who like computers, who use them at home, or who work in technical services. In order for the project to be successful, all staff members need to be included. The level of involvement will differ with some being part of the decision-making team while others may be included only in informational meetings. The higher the level of involvement, the better the chance of success.

2. Staff member as project director.

Although individual abilities and work responsibilities must be taken into consideration, in most cases it is desirable to choose a staff member as the project director. After the selection is made, clearly outline the responsibilities and the level of decision making authority.

3. Train staff in continuing technologies.

"Train me on the new computer and then I am done" is the training plan used by too many organizations. Emphasize at every opportunity that technology and change are a continuum, not a stop at a fixed point. Try not to sell your new technology with the argument that "if you fund this project it will last for ten years and it's all we will need." The day your new equipment is installed there will become available a different piece of equipment that performs more functions faster, cheaper, and in a more flexible, superior way. That is the nature of the change and technological cycles. Neither will ever be a fixed point but always a continuum. The sooner that is understood by the people with whom you work and the people who have a role in your project, the easier it will be. If you or your staff looks for one piece of equipment to solve all of the library's problems, the greater the disappointment when the neighboring library six months later buys the next generation system that does three new functions. A lot of wasted anxiety can be spent wringing hands and saying, "If I'd only waited." It is better to talk about technological and equipment development as a constantly evolving cycle. Tell your project partners or committee members right away that you will be seeking technology that you can afford now, use now, and have it improve you functionally as well as improve services to patrons while at the same time acknowledging that better technology will come along. A library director was overheard saying, "Buy something, use the hell out of it, don't ever regret it, improve service, and begin planning to buy again."

4. Protect staff from nonproductive work.

Any time a project of any kind from weeding the collection, to a fund-raiser, to adding a new service is undertaken, the temptation is to think that the new project can be added to the already heavy workload. Often little consideration is given to each member's overall workload and responsibilities. Following is an easy technique for getting rid of nonproductive work so there will be time for the new project.

Have the staff person list in priority order the ten most important activities in which they invest their work time. Review the list. Consider dropping the bottom two or three. Consider the consequences to the patrons if you did. Consider the list again when you are assigning and dividing tasks for the automation project.

5. Continually reinforce staff.

The library's past track record in dealing with change will gauge the amount of time you will need to spend reinforcing the staff about the value of new technology. Try not to sell new machines as a way to reduce staff work. Rather promote the value of improved service to patrons. If there are no benefits to the public, reevaluate the reasons behind the proposed change.

6. Consider future staff needs.

The average tenure for a professional librarian you hire today is twenty-two years. That means that the person you hire in 1996 most likely will stay at your information center until 2018. And that is just the average. Consider not only what knowledge, skills, and abilities you need in your newly hired staff for today but also what traits staff should have which will help them be able to be productive in the twenty-first century. If most of the circulation functions will be performed by self-service machines and the patrons will be able easily to do basic reference for themselves, what work will be left for the staff? Staff will need to make judgments and decisions and to provide in-depth reference and information work. In the near future, more staff time will be spent studying public demand and modifying the library selection profile rather than reviewing and ordering materials in case they might be needed.

During the job interview ask questions to elicit the applicant's thoughts concerning the future and his or her potential role in it. Asking an applicant "to describe one or two significant changes of which he or she is proud" leads you to discover whether he or she has been responsible for any changes. Questions about the applicant's personal methods of going about implementing change lets you know before you hire a person whether or not he or she considers him/herself as a person who creates (or abhors) change.

7. Productive conference/workshop attendance fosters positive change.

Most libraries, boards, and principals recognize the value of continuing education for the staff. Many libraries have full-scale inhouse staff development programs. Other libraries take advantage of consortia, networks, university, state libraries, or other continuing education programs. During a technology change it is additionally important to use the staff development opportunities wisely. Sometimes a workshop speaker gives the same message you wanted to give but your message has fallen on deaf ears. The workshop speaker is listened to because he or she does not appear to have any vested interest in the specific proposed change. Consider sending only one staff member to a specific class as a way of taking advantage of the widest variety of opportunities available. Make sure that the attendee is encouraged to share and report back to the rest of the staff. Consider sending other than the expected person to the workshop. A technical service staff member going to a public service class or a public service staff member going to a technical service workshop each has the potential of gaining new insights. Each staff member will bring a different and often unique perspective to the learning opportunity.

8. Willingness to trust and be open is a crucial value.

As networks continue to grow, more interdependences are created. As consortia/network memberships give added value to the service provided, databases, reference sources, and unique items will continue to be shared. Increasingly it is necessary to trust your consortium partners. When you join a group and provide access to your materials to those outside of your primary service clientele, you have to be able to ensure that each member will continue to provide his or her part of the network services. This trust is particularly important in networks/consortia that emphasize cooperative collection building. If you deemphasize buying/collecting/storing materials in a specific subject area because another member library has promised (sometimes even by contract) that it will continue to purchase/collect/preserve and retain materials in the subject area you discontinued, you must trust the library not only to make that commitment but also to continue it. Openness also allows you to make the bold decision to say it is all right to not attempt to collect everything because you are trusting other institutions to provide pieces of your patrons' collection information needs. Recruit people who are open and you can trust. Enter into consortial joint agreements with people who are open and you can trust.

9. Good, careful planning is the key to avoiding resistance.

After you have decided to make a change and you have reviewed the many factors that come into play in making a change, it is helpful if you can understand some of the reasons for resistance ahead of time. In 1992, Walter Giesbrect and Roberta McCarthy did a study of "Why Library Staff Resist the Use of CD-ROMs as a Reference Information Source." They found the most frequently given reasons were:

1. psychological (just didn't like change no matter what it was);
2. problems of multiple interfaces of various CD-ROM products (thought patrons not capable of using different search modes for different products);
3. increased teaching load (viewed the new technology as something that they had to explain more rather than a machine that helped to ease their workload);

4. increased costs (measured paper product costs vs CD-ROM produced costs without factoring in any improved access or more successful searches gaining more information for the patrons);
5. increased stress;
6. time required to learn new products (every new reference book or new magazine also requires time to learn how to use it and find the information located within it) and,
7. hardware/software issues (staff can find objections to any and every kind of hardware and software as we all have our favorites to use).[6]

Except for the specific equipment issues, most of the above seven issues could be listed as reasons to resist any change. See page 20–23 as these are similar to the resistance factors listed as common signals of any change resistance.

10. Recruit people who embrace change.

Do not only look for new staff who can deal with change. If possible, recruit staff members who not only accept the change continuum but actually embrace it. Look for "change agents"—those who thrive on change in order to provide improved and enhanced service to the library's patrons. Change still must be seriously and carefully considered, and should be not encouraged just because something is new and/or different. Look for new staff and encourage your existing staff to be open to changes that will add value to what service you are already providing or to those that will reach more of your potential patrons.

Consider your existing staff and try to understand their love or fear of change. Talk about change with them and try daily to get them to view change, particularly technological change, as part of an ever-changing continuum. The only thing that is constant is that there will always be change. Tom Miller, a principal of New Media Resources, a San Francisco-based consulting and acquisitions-search firm, spent the last five years in strategic level research and product development at Ziff Communications Company and Information Access Company, suggests eight specific tips for gearing up to become an electronic librarian.

1. Just do it—overcome your natural fears. Set a plan and plunge ahead.
2. Decide how information can help you achieve your institution's mission. When you have a clear understanding of you organization's goals, then you can determine

the new delivery systems necessary to meet those needs.
3. Develop your rationale—why will the information help?
4. Get some technology background—not only additional personal knowledge but also forming alliances with other technological people.
5. Introduce the technology.
6. Set up a pilot.
7. Gear up for training—shift in role from being a doer to being a doer *and* a facilitator.
8. Hang on. Life is going to get interesting.[7]

There is no apparent reason to fear librarians will be replaced. Sixty percent of the librarians in the Fisher study[8] said that end-user activity had actually increased library activity and produced more requests for complex searches and introduced new patrons to the library.

After evaluating staff considerations, it is necessary to review your existing or planned building. Only after these two reevaluations will you have the knowledge needed to proceed in developing a technology plan.

LIBRARY BUILDINGS IN AN AGE OF VIRTUAL REALITY

The Harold Washington Chicago Public Library, which opened in October 1991, has 70.1 miles of shelving for 1.7 million books. In addition, the Chicago Public Library contains millions of periodicals, microforms, pamphlets, and music. It covers one city block and contains 756,630 square feet on ten floors. The size of the building was determined first in 1922 when the first building plan was written. Changes in political leaders, the economy, struggles over location, and Chicago politics all kept the building from being completed for sixty-nine years. Although much of the building shelving is filled, in certain areas such as government documents, many areas are empty as most of the information is provided in non-book format.

The General Service Agency of the United States Government, which publishes thousands of reports and specifications yearly, is transferring its information from hard copy to optical storage mediums. Their plans call for their information dissemination process to be totally paperless by 1997. This is just one example of a shift in information storage demands.

The Urban Libraries Council 1994 study of their eighty-nine member libraries showed an anticipated decrease in print on paper formats in urban libraries from 86 percent in 1990 to 69 percent by the year 2000.

FIGURE 4.2 **Trends in Materials Expenditures in Urban Libraries**			
	Print on Paper	Electronic	Audio-Visual
1990	86%	4%	10%
2000	69%	18%	13%[9]

Michael Crichton in his novel *Disclosure* vividly describes a virtual filing system. Virtual help angels provide guidance through the files which appear to be hanging in midair. Reading pages 115-117 and 350-359 of this novel will introduce you to a virtual filing system. Seeing the movie (with the same title) also helps one visualize a virtual filing system.

When librarians first started talking about virtual libraries they were using the term "virtual" to mean "not there"; as in the patron was in one location and the material was being piped in from another location. The first true "virtual" library was tried in Australia. No physical materials were purchased—all information was purchased for electronic access. They bought access to online periodicals, purchased all the resource materials that were available on CD-ROM, and connected to OCLC to locate hard copy materials held in libraries worldwide. They also digitized core materials so they could be accessible online.

Other people, such as library consultant Rob McGee, talk about the digitized library and the transition from print sources to digital sources. In a virtual library everything is connected to information located somewhere else. In a digital library most of the information is still located in the same place or may be located remotely but is available in a machine-readable format.

The filing system that Crichton describes, however, is not just a super online filing system. It is one in which the image of a file cabinet is there and it looks like a file cabinet and the documents look like regular paper files. If you reached out and touched the files, you would touch air. Could you create a virtual reality package where you could pick your own reading setting? You could consider the comfy, pillowed window seats of your neighborhood, or Carnegie Library's Children's Room, or perhaps the magnificent recently renovated Library of Congress Reading Room, the British Museum Reading Room, the library of your school, or a recreation of your home library setting. Do you have to be in the actual building to get the warm, fuzzy book comfort level or could you be in the location of your choice and through virtual reality imaging be in your favorite library?

Paper is still the most convenient delivery medium. Paper can be delivered and received everywhere. There are no hardware requirements with paper. The fewer the electronic delivery sites, the more attractive paper becomes. Any kind of hardware requirements, even the cheapest and simplest, reduces the number of delivery sites. In order to replace paper you must do two things: 1) maximize delivery sites; and 2) minimize hardware requirements. This is exactly what Bill Gates is proposing with his new total earth coverage satellite grid. He and an associate, Craig McCaw, have applied for a patent to put into place globe covering satellites which would provide cheap access for third world countries as well as people who live too far down the road for the cable companies to make a profit.

Will monuments to knowledge like the Carnegie libraries of old become elegant edifices containing empty rooms? Continuing to build bigger and expanded libraries regardless of type has been a goal of most librarians. More shelf space was constantly needed not only to warehouse the older archival materials but the part of the 30,000+ books published each year that the library could afford to purchase. Few questioned the idea that libraries were almost always too small. This dilemma may finally pass as electronic resources supplant many paper ones.

Reviewing the phases of automation in relation to buildings reveals some interesting factors.

1. Automate what you did yesterday—Most libraries have completed this stage. Technical services space needs were reduced in many cases. Cabling and conduit were added and additional workstations were placed throughout buildings.
2. What you do changes—processes change; methods and procedures change. Most of the byproducts of these changes consume less space. Compare the space required to house the thousands of check-out cards in even a medium-sized library to the reduced space necessary to house a computer work station.
3. Transformation of library—The library's role redefined and sharpened to concentrate on what the institution can do best, taking advantage of new technology to strengthen and enhance its role. Information is available on demand when the need presents itself, not in anticipation of demand as in the past. Fax machines, computer terminals, and other multifunction machines are

interspersed throughout the library. Phone books contain dial-in access lines for public information. This is a time of blended collections and blended technologies.

WHAT EFFECT DOES AUTOMATION HAVE ON BUILDING PLANNING?

According to Susan Baerg Epstein, there are three keys to building planning in the twenty-first century.[10]

1. Enough electricity
2. Telecommunications ability
3. Flexibility

Although wireless technology is beginning to play an increasingly important role in providing library services, new buildings should plan to have a strong electrical backbone throughout the building and allow for the possibility that the communications within an area may be wireless. The amount of space necessary to shelve hard copies of books and magazines will decrease dramatically. Refer to your collection development plan when determining how much shelf space will be needed.

BLENDED LIBRARIES

A blended library is one that takes full advantage of providing information via many technologies while still meeting the patrons' needs for information in hard copy. A blended library has a comfortable, casual reading area with current magazines and bestsellers along with rows of computer terminals to connect to the global information network. The new San Francisco Public Library is an example of a monumental building with a blended interior. Over 600 public service terminals are available to the public. By the year 2000 public service terminals are expected to furnish every home, school, and business with twenty-four hour dial-in access to the San Francisco Public Library's resources. The check-out system features a smart card for patron self check-in and -out of books and materials. Their planning team is working closely with commercial companies in three areas to provide enhanced service.

1) An imaging system to preserve important paper documents and materials that are deteriorating and to expand access to the huge photograph collection.
2) An interactive multimedia function that will allow multimedia resources located in the library to be easily retrieved over phone lines at the patron's location of choice.

FIGURE 4.3 Digitization not only preserves photographs like this one, but also expands their accessibility by making them available over networks and the World Wide Web.

3) An electronic browser for scanning text and images from online or CD-ROM sources is available in one of six languages.

Several other libraries have created blended libraries. The award-winning Purcellville Public Library (Loudon County, Virginia) is one example. Computer workstations are placed throughout the library. There is a comfortable reading area and multimedia area. The Purcellville Library paid particular attention to network design, cable, and wiring infrastructure that allows for flexibility and expansion. Blended libraries will be further discussed in the next chapter.

NOTES

1. Sineath, Timothy W., ed. Library and Information Science Education Statistical Report, 75, 107. Sarasota, Florida: Association for Libraries and Information Science Education, 1990.
2. Sparks, Martha Evans. "Time out from technology: a fresh look at subliminal recruiting for librarianship." *Southeastern Librarian* (Winter, 1994):87.
3. Touby, Lauren. "The New Librarian is an info-surfer." *Glamour*, vol. 92 issue 4 (April 1994):126.
4. McClenney, Elizabeth Gail. "Why students choose careers in Information and Library Science: factors that affect the decision process." Unpublished master's research paper, University of North Carolina at Chapel Hill, School of Information and Library Science 1989, pp. 8, 9, 28.
5. Rose, Ernestine. *The Public Library in American Life.* New York: Columbia University Press, 1954, p. 76.
6. Giesbrect, Walter and Roberta McCarthy. *CD-ROM Professional*, 4:3 (May 1991):34–38.
7. Miller, Tom. "How to become an Electronic Librarian." *Information Today* (February, 1995):40, 41.
8. Fisher, Jean, and Bjorner, Susanne. *Special Libraries* (**no title, in info section**) vol. 85, no. 4 (Fall 1994):281–291.
9. "Collection Development Survey Results." Urban Libraries Council Fast Facts Series (June 1994):4.
10. Epstein, S.B. "Technology, Buildings and the Future." *Library Journal*, Vol 116 Issue 22 (December 1991):112.

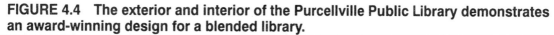

FIGURE 4.4 The exterior and interior of the Purcellville Public Library demonstrates an award-winning design for a blended library.

FIGURE 4.4 (cont.)

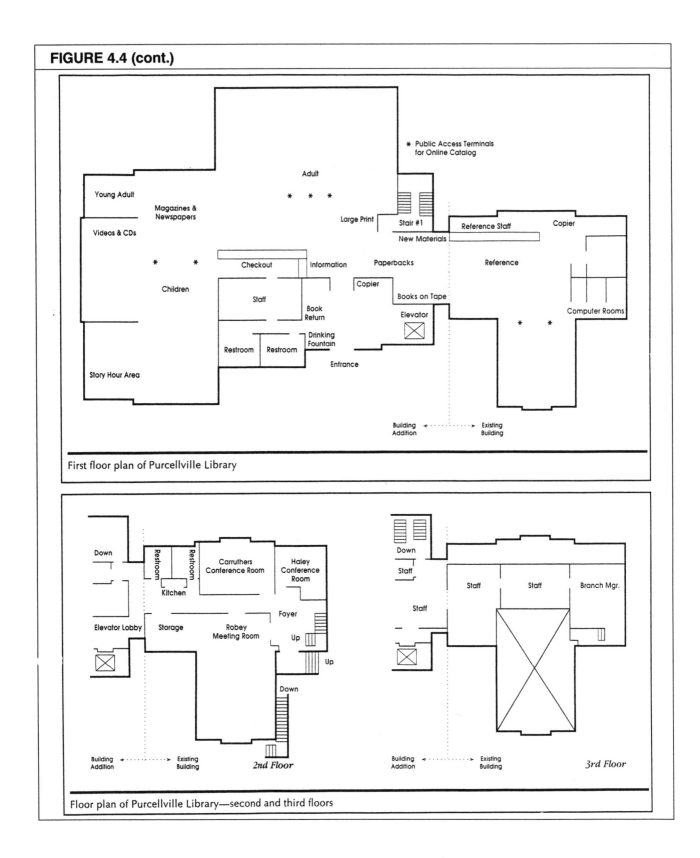

First floor plan of Purcellville Library

Floor plan of Purcellville Library—second and third floors

5 LIBRARY OPPORTUNITIES: TECHNO-CONVERGENCE

People love packages. People like to have control. The VCR gives people control over when they watch television programs. Individuals are no longer dependent on the television programmers' time schedules. People can choose their own time to watch shows. The VCR allows time shifting. Some of the more recent technologies allow not only *time* shifting but *place* shifting. Information previously was place bound, usually within the library walls. With the focus on new opportunities through new technology comes increased conflict and competition. States and nations as well as many diverse industries are competing with each other to be the first to capture the economic benefits of the technologies as well as take advantage of declining telecommunications costs. Why is there so much convergence now? The competition is among the print, telephone, and cable industries; the movie and video industries are also highly competitive.

COMPETITION DRIVES CONVERGENCE

States see a coordinated telecommunication infrastructure as necessary to the economic development of their state. States are taking diverse paths. Some states are developing and supporting use of technology to improve educational opportunities such as distance learning. Other states see the advantage of high speed data networks that help research activities both in the public and private sectors. Some states are using their advanced telecommunications networks to entice new business and industry. Several states have totally funded the construction of their statewide telecommunications infrastructure. Almost all states have or are preparing a plan for a statewide network.

Competition is also rampant among countries. Smaller countries with monopolistic communication systems already have been able to complete their county's ISDN (Integrated Services Digital Network) system. Great Britain, France, and Germany have had countrywide ISDN systems for several years. The Integrated Services Digital Network allows data, voice, and video images to be transmitted over the same phone line at the same time. Japan has committed to having ISDN in every business and home by the end of the century and has initiated programs that will support the development of "smart cities" and create regional information hubs that can serve as administrative centers and platforms for economic growth.

What does techno-convergence have to do with libraries? Public access is what is at stake. As commercial and entertainment ventures proliferate, the public interest is in peril. The public library must continue to guard the public's access to information. As the new National Information Infrastructure (NII) is created, librarians will have an opportunity to implement critical public policy goals. Will the public library become a place for those who can't afford computers?

Pat O'Brien, Director of the Alexandria [Virginia] Public Library suggested during a mock debate about the future of the public library, "It isn't even necessary to maintain a public library as a place for the information poor." His tongue-in-cheek suggestion at the 1994 PLA Meeting was to give out information stamps similar to food stamps. The economically deprived could use the info-stamps to purchase information from commercial services which would provide information about jobs, government benefits, and social service agencies as easily and/or efficiently as the library.

Maintaining free access to information will continue to be one of the many important roles for the library. According to Richard A. Bowers, President of Optical Publishing Association, most Americans get their information from five main sources:

1) Friends and family;
2) business/professional acquaintances;
3) vendors;
4) public libraries; and
5) government.[1]

It is important to maintain the public part of these sources. It is interesting to speculate what will happen when a 500-channel television becomes an economically feasible reality. Will the information sources change?

Since recent legislative and regulatory changes now allow cross-technology distribution of information, techno-convergence has become more intertwined. Some of the company mergers created single-owned markets of 30-40 million homes. Telephone, cable, and print companies are going head-to-head to get the most market share possible.

The telephone company encourages the sharing of the telecommunication infrastructure, including cable cross ownership and incentives to support accelerated deployment of new technology. The phone companies argue that their ideas would help to create a telecommunications structure that is competitive with other states and countries and would create more jobs. If the development of the fiber-based broad band telecommunications network were accelerated, the phone companies anticipate great benefits that would not only impact consumers but also businesses of all kinds as well as the overall economy.

The newspaper industry does not support the telephone companies' proposals. Newspapers have a lot to gain by maintaining and not sharing control over the information they distribute. Many newspapers are diversifying into online and interactive phone services. "Access Atlanta" is the online twenty-four hour access to the *Atlanta Journal-Constitution*. Not only does it provide online access to the wire service news as it comes in but also to bulletin boards, information about what's going on in Atlanta, tourist attractions, and job notices before they come out in the print version and ready reference services. Depending on the ownership of a newspaper and its interest in providing online consumer paid access, some newspapers are less opposed to the blending of the technologies than they were previously.

The cable companies were also opposed to allowing telephone companies the opportunity to provide video and information services. One of the cable companies' main oppositions is their belief that with the large amounts of capital available to the telephone companies, they could eliminate competition and also reduce the public's freedom of choice.

The telephone companies' response to these issues is that the newspaper and cable companies are afraid of competition. Phone companies feel that with appropriate regulations, consumers still can expect reasonable rates for universal basic services.

Cable operators are entering the wireless service market. The cable market is one of the quickest growing parts of the telecommunications industry. They are working to bypass companies that target very high-volume, low-cost voice and data business traffic. Bypass companies link local businesses with branch offices and long distance companies using a fiber optic network. This process allows cable operators to avoid the higher costs associated with residential services. Telephone companies are left then to provide the higher-cost services.

Cable operators also are entering the personal data communication service market. Cable systems are used to link PDA pocket telephone to the public phone network from almost anywhere in the United States. Phone calls across the country using cable television facilities are being transmitted by some cable companies.[2]

The cable modem is a new product that allows cable television systems to provide fast network data transmission. The cable modem has allowed the cable industry to become a major player in the information delivery arena. Since there is no standards organization for cable modems, the devices will not be able to communicate with modems made by anyone else. With the growing availability of speedy ISDN lines, cable transmission speed does not compare favorably. Security of information sent over cable lines would be a problem as cable television systems are a broadcast medium, not a secure network. Cable line transmission may meet your local needs, but carefully consider the needs of your network and its users.

In the near future, all of the competing industries will jockey for position and market share. Use of the Internet by so many individuals is also being noted by all of the competing players. Because all of these information delivery technologies affect libraries, every effort should be made to keep abreast of the ever-shifting developments.

TECHNO-CONVERGENCE AND LIBRARY USERS

When parlors were built in houses, they were used for entertaining company or formal family events requiring extra space. When radios were introduced in the 1920s, they were placed in the parlor and the family and guests sat in the formal area listening to the radio shows. When television was introduced, it usually was placed in the living room in a central place of honor in a large ornate wooden console. The television was a major piece of furniture and chairs and sofas were grouped around it. When computers first came into homes, most of them were placed in the den or office. Since the average American family has four radios and two television sets, these appliances have moved into many other rooms in the house, including the garage and outdoor areas. The interactive television developers and marketers are hoping to move the television and the computer into the family room in one single unit. The question is—will people who use computers in their work want to have television sets or PCs as focal points in their homes? Will people who view television as recreation and a computer as work want to have one blended unit with elements of both? What role will the telephone play in bringing nonpersonal information into the home?

A possible library response to the confusion reigning with the various technologies is to ensure that all library products are user friendly. Before you make a decision about a new technology, try it out on your patrons. Vendors often will allow patrons as well as staff to try a product. Let patrons and students fill out the same evaluation sheets as the staff. Review and factor in their comments. If the product is not favorably reviewed by your patrons, talk with them and try to find ways to overcome the negatives. Consider forming a patron group for ongoing review. Improving patron service should be the first and overriding goal of a library. Continued attention should be paid to patron reactions to any changes you make including technological changes. About six to eight weeks before you will be making a change, post the change. Try to state the wording in the most positive way. Below is one suggested way:

> In order to better serve you in the future _____
> _____
> If you have any questions, ask.

The most user-friendly change still will not be enthusiastically received if one day things are one way and the next day the patron finds everything changed. Most people are not comfortable with change. You have to work to overcome their discomfort every step of the way.

THE LIBRARY AS A PLACE TO INTRODUCE NEW TECHNOLOGY

Another role that the library should play now and in the future is as a place to introduce new technology. Again, that does not mean that a library should embrace every new technology and discard all previous ones. As the library is a place where new ideas are introduced, could the library not be also a place where people could come and try new technology so it would lose some of its mystique? When the library does then adopt that same technology, the introduction would be easier. This is not to suggest that the library should become a vendor showcase or a commercial showroom. Instead consider that a display explaining personal data assistants with information about their use, which includes many different brands, might help non-users to discover the library as a place that showcases and explains new technology. Lecture series could be presented to complement the displays.

THE LIBRARY AS AN INTERNET CONNECTION

The Internet has changed the method many people use to get information as well as the way many libraries provide information. In 1994 more than 77 percent of university libraries, 84 percent of public libraries with operating budgets higher than $5 million, and 21 percent of all public libraries provided Internet access.[3] Many states have statewide projects that provide an Internet connection to every school. The 1994 report, *Public Libraries and the Internet: Study Results, Policy Issues, and Recommendations* found that most public librarians agree that

1. public libraries should provide Internet access to patrons;
2. public libraries should serve as a safety net for public access to the Internet;
3. public libraries should provide Internet access without charge; and
4. future monetary support of public libraries is integrally linked to the Internet.[4]

Due to inexpensive linkup charges, even the smallest library can participate in the resource-rich Internet. Remember that the Internet is always open and offers very current information.

If you currently are not connected to the Internet, visit a neighboring library that is connected—better yet, visit several. Talk with the staff to find out firsthand about the advantages and disadvantages of using this resource. Ask about their initial reactions as well as their current perceptions. Try using the Internet yourself. Pretend you are a patron with a specific question. With help from the experienced staff, try to find the answer (or answers) to that question. Post a query on STUMPERS and have the library staff send you the responses. Then, just try browsing the Internet as you would browse up and down the aisles of a library.

If the library at which you experiment also has access to the World Wide Web, you could pay a virtual visit to Washoe County (Nevada) Library's Cyber-Library. The WWW is, among other things, a multi-media Internet database. More computer power is required to enable its advanced graphics, sound, and full-motion video. You can dial into Washoe County at http://www.washoe.lib.nv.us. The Cyber-Library is arranged quite like a regular physical facility. A menu of choices provides many options. It starts with a home page (the WWW term for a menu) including a listing of branch libraries (with their hours and maps) as well as library program and policy information.

The "Bookstacks" contain the electronic text of 850 books that can either be downloaded or read at the workstation. Another menu choice is "Children's Room." Here illustrated children's books can be viewed and read. The "Local Information Center" contains highway conditions, weather information and forecasts, satellite photographs, and a current listing of area events. "Map Room" links to a large collection of digitized maps at the University of Texas at Austin. "Periodicals Room" puts a user into the UnCover Journal Service. A Reno home page offering the entire Reno Municipal Code as well as detailed information on the Reno City Council can be found in the "Government Documents Room." The "Reference Desk" links to Internet reference sources that are available through Web browsers. Examples include language dictionaries, *Bartlett's Familiar Quotations*, and the *CIA World Fact Book*. Another menu choice is "Gateway to Other Libraries." This path leads to the University of Nevada and the University of California catalogs as well as the Library of Congress and a wide selection of libraries of all types. An Internet access service, Power Net, located in Reno, provided the service. According to Washoe County Library Director Nancy Cummings, "At a total cost of $55 per month, this lets the Library offer a wide range of resources to 15,000 Internet users in Washoe County and around the world."[5] The Internet Branch is available to people all over the world who have an Internet connection.

Another example of a library using the Internet and the Web to expand access to its services is the New York Public Library's home page. Users electronically explore the resources of the Library, its four research centers, and eighty-two neighborhood branches. Library President Paul LeClerk described this new development as follows: "Now as the Library enters its second century, we view the Web as an invaluable new tool in the further globalization of the New York Public Library, its collections, and services."[6]

Try looking up library home pages in your state and/or region. Look at CNN Interactive News (http://www.cnn.com). Every day libraries create new home pages and/or link their local resources to the Web to create locally customized access to Net resources and make local resources available globally. Many useful facts and sources are identified in *Washington Online: How to Access the Federal Government on the Internet*. This book contains the addresses and in-depth descriptions of about 300 federal Internet sites and outlines their resources.

Many library-related products are being sold through the Internet. In a blending of technological applications, Voyager, a premier CD-ROM production company, sells CD-ROM and laser discs via its Web page. They have found the Internet to be a promising retail outlet. You can review their products on their Web page (http://www.voyagerco.com). Many bookstores sell books and electronic versions of books over the Internet. It is estimated that there are over 300 booksellers on the Internet.[7] Some have nothing more than a home page banner and a database of book listings. Others have dazzling graphics and are a kind of cyber-coffeeshop, part bookstore, part library, and part bazaar. Carnegie Mellon University has set up a book publishers' and retailers' home page as a jumpsite that launches users into a potpourri of book sites. This platform links a wide range of Internet booksellers' and publishers' catalogs. The address is http://thyle.mt.cs.cmu.edu:8001/bookstores. Many other products and services are sold through the Internet, often by enticing buyers with free offers. One such free trial offer is for Newspage—try it at http://www.newspage.com. Magazines are migrating to the Internet. Called e-zines, there are already hundreds of electronic magazines that can be read online.

To help navigate through the often confusing paths of the Internet, the number of helpful resources increases daily. *Internet World*, a mildly technical monthly journal contains tips, news, and evaluations as well as indepth articles. Since 1993, *Library Journal* has included an Internet column. *American Libraries*' Internet Librarian column offers folksy, easy-to-understand advice on the Net by cybrarian Karen G. Schneider.

THE LIBRARY AS A TEACHING CENTER

Technological innovation allows library patrons to use the library as a learning place. Although libraries of all types have traditionally included teaching and learning in their goals or missions, as budgets were continually cut, many libraries cut or decreased the importance of their teaching role.

New, cost-effective technology could expand the library's role in teaching. In the area of language training there are many improved products. Libraries—both school and public—can circulate Berlitz Spanish and French language translators that are available to be played on Nintendo, hand-held Gameboys. Many user-friendly, inexpensive, English-as-a-second-language software packages are available that include online dictionaries, interactive drills, and games.

The American Association of School Librarians developed ICONnect, a technology initiative to get students, librarians, media specialists, and teachers connected to learn using the Internet. ICONnect resources will help students to develop the information and visual literacy skills they need to be productive citizens and provide library media specialists and teachers with training to navigate the Internet. AASL past president, Jacqueline

Mancall, said about the project, "Through ICONnect, we want to position the school library media program as the central of the educational program in a school and to establish a coordinated network of library media specialists able to meet the information needs of students . . . "[8] Electronic field trips (simulating traditional field trips via a combination of linear video, CD-ROM, and narrowband online services) could be taken from the school media center. By reading library literature other similar projects can be identified which will enhance the library's role in teaching.

THE LIBRARY AS A CULTURAL CENTER

Another role for the library in the future is the library as cultural center. Many libraries throughout the United States are focusing on this role right now. Some people believe that the cultural role will be the only one left for the public library, but through this cultural preservationist role, the public library will continue to exist. CARL's Rebecca Lenzini stated at the 1993 North American Serials Interest Group (NASIG) meeting during a session on the role of the library in 2020 that she honestly felt there would be not much left for libraries as we know them today to do in 2020. The one role she did think would be sustained and continue to be publicly funded was the public library's role in preserving and maintaining our culture, both through collecting, preserving, and maintaining cultural artifacts and through outreach programming to share various cultures with others. One example of the library as cultural center is the old Chicago Public Library Building, which has been restored and made into a cultural center. It contains, among many other significant collections, the Museum of Broadcast Journalism. Many permanent collections as well as traveling exhibits are displayed there year-round. A full schedule of guest lectures and subject experts complements the exhibits. It is somewhat difficult to imagine that by the year 2020 the cultural center will be thriving but at the same time the 756,630 square foot block-long Harold Washington Library would no longer be in operation. In an already accomplished conversion similar to Chicago's, the Birmingham Public Library converted its old building into the Linn-Henley Southern History Research Center. A large meeting room is home to many cultural activities including a well-attended Jazz Festival.

Special collections are often attached to academic libraries. It is interesting to think of a time when the special collections will be the academic library's main and/or only focus because the rest of the materials located within the library could be obtained over the Internet or other online sources. Other large city libraries have magnificent museums attached to them. Often the museums contain large collections of photographs, many of which are deteriorating. Photodigitizing and image scanning allow for easy preservation of the photographs. Once the photo has been scanned and digitized, it also can be pressed onto a CD-ROM and that CD-ROM can be sold and distributed for much wider use of the specialized materials. Many libraries are involved in photo digitization projects. The Atlanta Public Library is continually scanning its huge, unique African-American history collection. Companies such as Kodak offer products for capturing, enhancing, editing, archiving, managing, publishing, and printing images.

HOME DELIVERY OF INFORMATION

Home delivery of information creates challenges for the librarian. Exploring possible outcomes to the challenges will help you view them as opportunities. As noted Technocat Craig Patchett is well-known for saying, "Wireless communications technology will advance to the point where PDAs [Personal Data Assistants] will be able to replace your fax machine, telephone, modem, library and eventually even your television set."

What brought about his vision? Changes in costs for mobile air time have been reduced by almost two-thirds over a period of a few years. The improvement in wireless technology combined with the dramatic price decreases have opened new doors to the use of wireless transmission for more than car and mobile house phone and status symbols for people on the go. Worldwide, one new telephone subscriber in six gets a mobile phone.[9]

A 1988 *Time* magazine article looked at the future in communications technology. The pictures accompanying the article showed people wearing eyeglasses with miniature antennas mounted on the corners. These goggled people of the future were surrounded by buildings and billboards which all had sprouted antennas. The picture had a comical aspect to it combined with science fiction. In 1994 antennas for cellular transmission were located about every half mile in most urban areas. In the near future, cities will be dotted with radio relay stations, however, the antennas will be smaller. They could be located on every office building, gas station, and highway exit sign.

The personal communicator concept is moving closer to reality and is available in selected cities. With the personal communicator concept every individual would have one unique number for access to phone, fax, computer, and pager. This number would not change when the person moved to a different house or took a different job or moved to a different city. With total wireless communication a person could be reached anywhere without requiring a direct connecting device. With this process, the information moves digitally; there is quicker and crisper transmission with better resolution. Currently, x-rays and blueprints, which are hard-to-transmit formats, are being sent successfully through phones which contain small screens. Japan has introduced a personal handphone system. Using small, low-powered base stations situated close together in large cities, Astel, a Japanese company, offers a telephone about the size of a powder compact. The local call on this unit costs less than equivalent calls placed from pay phones.

There are three types of wireless technology. The first type of wireless technology is the one with which many people are familiar—cellular technology. Using cellular technology, the wireless telephone service transmits calls in a non-computerized form via radio towers located in small areas known as cells. The handset typically only handles voice transmission. Cellular technology is available in nearly every city and town but in the rural areas coverage is spotty. The closer the user is to the cell the better the transmission. Conversely, the farther away the caller is from the cell, the poorer the transmission. In some cases when the distance becomes too great, transmission will cease altogether. There are 15 million cellular customers nationwide and as transmission range improves the customer base will continue to grow. Cellular modems are also available in large urban markets.

The second type of wireless technology is PCS or Personal Communication Service. This technology uses wireless phones that transmit calls over radio frequencies. The radio frequencies were auctioned in May, 1994. The competitors have not yet sorted out which company will own the dominant market share. The telephone handset can handle voice, phone mail, and data communications. The PCS concept is currently in use in London and is being tested in some markets in the United States. Seattle is one of those new markets.

Seattle car drivers are testing a new wireless traffic information system that sends down signals over spare space on the FM radio signals. The system is run by a consortium including IBM, General Motors' Delco, Japan's Seiko, and Washington State's Department of Transportation. Remember the watch that provided Dick Tracy with special information that gave him the edge over his pursuers? This system is very similar. The project features a wristwatch worn while driving the car that will warn of accidents ahead, car radios that would guide you to an alternate route, and laptop computers that display maps showing how fast traffic is moving on other roads. The Federal Government eventually wants to set up a similar program nationwide. The three features of the Seattle test include:

1. Watches. Seiko already is selling its message watch in some areas of the county. It has a tiny two-line display screen and can receive electronic signals over FM frequencies including weather, paging messages, and sports scores. The message watch being used in the Seattle test also will pick up traffic bulletins, beeping when one is arriving. Data is transmitted as subcarrier signals by FM radio stations that Seiko has around the world.
2. Car radios. A new GM Delco car radio includes a two-line display screen and the ability to track where the car is by bouncing signals off a satellite. This radio could guide a driver around traffic jams as well as provide a reception source for paging messages.
3. Computers. Small console-attached computers display a map showing where you are and how traffic is moving around your location. If a road flashes green on the screen, it is moving. If it flashes red, it is jammed up.

Estimated costs for setting up the project are low—about $5 to $7 million—because all of the pieces are in place. The consortium is working to connect these parts into an integrated system. A goal for the project is to price the system low so that many drivers will purchase it and help the flow of traffic.

The third type of wireless technology is SMR or Specialized Mobile Radio. This technology uses wireless phones to transmit computerized signals over frequencies used for taxi dispatch. The user has one handset for voice plus two-way paging, messages, phone mail, and data communication when hooked up to a laptop computer. SMR is currently in full use in Los Angeles and in some forty-five of the fifty United States markets.

The total number of wireless subscribers is projected to have tremendous growth and to continue to grow through the beginning of the century. What do cellular phones have to do with providing library service? One project that combines cellular technology and the use of a PDA (Personal Data Assistant) is the University of South Alabama Library's (Mobile, Alabama) Library Without a Roof Project. This was the first library to provide public access catalog on a hand-held computer using cellular communications. Three companies worked together on this project: AT&T, Bell South Cellular, and Notable Technologies.

Project Director Dale Foster said, "Much has been made of the virtual library or the library without walls. This project takes the concept one step further. The success of this preliminary study shows the ability of researchers to access a library catalog, electronic mail, or read the entire works of Shakespeare in electronic form while sitting under a tree in the park. Researchers are no longer bound by the physical walls of a library building, indeed they do not even need an office or a telephone.[10]

The PDA that was used in the project was the EO of AT&T, a notebook sized computer which included a cellular phone/modem. The EO uses handwriting recognition technology similar to the childhood toy Etch-A-Sketch. The user writes on the computer screen using a magnetic pen. The PDA translates the handwriting into machine-readable text. The software, developed by Notable Technologies, Inc., allows the users to communicate directly with remote mainframe computers. The users were able to access SOUTHCAT (the library's online public access catalog), DIALOG Information Services, OCLCs FirstSearch, LEXIS/NEXIS, read electronic mail, and navigate the Internet.

For fun, to show the usefulness of the technology, the project demonstrator sat by a lake on campus to visually illustrate the point of the library without a roof. Besides the convenience and novelty offered by the technology, the project explored practical uses in both educational and library environments. The economics of local area networks and cellular communication links to mainframe computers are being explored to discover ways to reduce the cost of expanding access to electronic information sources.

The AT&T EO Personal Data Assistant was made available on the commercial market in 1993. It was the largest of the PDAs available. It took a great deal of effort to implement the handwriting recognition system. It was the only PDA at the time, however, to include a cellular phone/modem which greatly enhanced its capabilities over other PDAs. Its enhanced capabilities made its price double the other PDAs. Due to its bulky size and high cost compared to other PDAs, AT&T took the EO unit off the market in spring, 1994, an extremely short but not unusual product cycle for new technology.

With this wireless technology no longer on the market, did the roof collapse on the library without a roof? The project is continuing but using another PDA which offers expanded features at a lesser cost and a smaller unit. Visit an office store or electronics boutique and try out the current PDA models featured. Each new unit has improvements and enhanced features.

OTHER NEW TECHNOLOGIES AND THEIR LIBRARY SERVICE APPLICATIONS

When you experiment with new technologies, expect that some of the products will have an exceptionally short product cycle. Enjoy the advantages and additional services of the new technology and also accept the fact that many of the products are rushed to market without all the bugs worked out. Continue to use what you purchase as long as you can. Do not consider the purchase a mistake because you did benefit from its new and/or time saving convenient features.

Another innovative use of wireless technology is Skyfax, a global wireless messaging system. It uses the "one number no matter where you are" concept. With the one toll-free number, clients and colleagues can send a person a fax even if they don't know where they are. Other similar services are available often utilizing satellite links. Xerox is promoting an open documents system that will "print anything, anywhere, anytime." As library patrons use such services, their expectations for what is available at the library will increase. New photocopy machines copy, scan, fax, collate, and staple; all these functions are controlled by software running on a desktop computer. The company's key goal is to reduce the steps needed to produce a document. In an office environment, a person can send a word processing file directly online for printing and copying. Since copy machines are so heavily used in libraries, could patrons save time with an online connection from the library's PAC to the Xerox machine?[11]

Blockbuster and IBM have teamed up to make a computerized system that would change the way recorded music is bought and sold. This production method was tested in a kiosk in Deerfield Beach, Florida. Music lovers could listen to a favorite song or group of songs and request that they be produced. A customized CD would be pressed within five to six minutes. The advantage to the store is that it would not keep any stock except for the most popular and best-selling CDs.

As technology changes and CD and/or digitizing costs drop dramatically, could libraries offer customized production of materials for patrons who want to retain information in some form other than hardcopy or remote access? Will people carry their 100 favorite books digitally encoded on credit card size smart cards?

The CD-ROM production market was driven by the CD audio market. Cheaper production methods were developed because the multimillion dollar CD audio market demanded them. If the on-site production of music CDs becomes economically feasible, it is possible that on-site CD-ROM production on demand might become practical in libraries.

Technological coalitions will become more prevalent as products continue to interact with each other in the chaotic business and technological environment. The library environment is also chaotic because there is no front-running solution at this time to the centralized or distributed delivery systems.

Speech recognition technology is another technology that will have an impact on libraries. There is a product out that would be every ready reference librarian's dream. You hum a few bars of the music and it recognizes the piece and gives you its name and composer. This is only one of the numerous library applications for speech recognition technology. Some Macintosh computers already respond to simple voice commands: edit, stop, start.

In another new partnership, IBM and Compton's New Media have joined together to develop several new voice recognition commercial products. Several of these have direct implications for libraries. The Sporting News is available using an IBM system called Command and Query. This technology allows 1,000 active words to be used from a base of 20,000 words. It can be used with a standard audio board. It does not require any specialized training. Voice commands that it would recognize are:

> Show me your player statistics
> Display your statistics
> Give me information on [a specific player]

The other voice recognition program IBM has developed besides Command and Query is Dictation. The Dictation program works with 32,000 active words from a total base of 100,000 words. It recognizes speech at speeds up to seventy words per minute. The program utilizes statistical models to differentiate between like sounding words, i.e., one/won, our/hour, and two/to/too. When this technology is commercially available, it would allow you to dictate notes to the computer which would print the words on the screen.

A commercial product that utilizes speech recognition is LAWTALK. This product is a joint venture of Westlaw and Kolvox Communications. It is comprised of a series of set commands that can be used with Westlaw. In order to use this program, a 486 PC with 16 mg RAM is necessary. This product differs from The Sporting News in that the LAWTALK created a personal voice file so that the more a person uses it, the better the program becomes at correctly recognizing your particular speech patterns. A disadvantage of this first generation system is that the user must pause one tenth of a second between each word for the system to recognize the words. There is some training time necessary to have this system be most productive. A well received feature of LAWTALK is its voice-activated document production system. The user can move entire sections of documents, save, and reuse them to notably reduce legal document production time.

Wireless keyboards are another new innovation. Several companies have products on the market. Laser technology, similar to television remote control, is used to beam keystrokes to a receiver on the computer. This is another step in the portability and flexibility of computer devices. There are commercial products that allow for data storage on a watch. One example was jointly developed by Timex and Microsoft. The Data Link Watch not only stores information in the watch, but also allows for downloading information from the PC directly into the watch. The watch is held up to the PC screen and a button is pressed on the keyboard. Information is then transferred in seconds. Available functions on the Data Link include appointments, phone numbers, special dates, alarms, time settings, and to-do lists. Although the watch is only 1 1/2" in diameter, the display comprises four easily readable lines.

ADOPTING AND ADAPTING NEW TECHNOLOGIES

Ambrose Bierce said, "The future is that time in which our affairs prosper, our friends are true and our happiness is assured." Although new technologies create tremendous opportunities, they do not assure our happiness.

In fall, 1988 during a presentation for the Virginia State Library, I predicted ten characteristics for the future of CD-ROMs in the 1990s. They were:

1. Hardware Innovation
2. Shorter Access Time
3. Faster Data Transfer Speeds
4. Improved Graphics
5. "Caching"—so multiple users can access the same disc in rapid succession
6. Re-writable Optical Discs
7. Improved Juke Boxes
8. Drives that Overwrite Data
9. Increased Standardization
10. Cost-effective Mastering Equipment for Library Use

When I created this list, I was thinking toward the late 1990s. Yet by 1993, all of these items were realities except for number eight, Drives that Overwrite Data. That technology took a different path. One of the roles that the library is likely to play in the future is that of publisher. Some libraries have been connected to the publishing business by publishing a library or local history. Libraries in the United Kingdom have long seen publishing as one of their traditional roles. That has not been the case in America. However, with the opportunity to cost-effectively produce CD-ROM products, the library can function more as a publisher and creator rather then just a collector, maintainer, and preserver.

In the early 1990s, mastering service bureaus opened which would produce CD-ROMs with small, limited distribution. It cost about $25,000 to replicate a disc. In 1993 cheap production equipment could be rented at $100 per day and a cost of $1.00 to $2.00 per disc to replicate. It was feasible to produce several hundred copies. Mastering of the first disc was $2,000. With the introduction of low-cost compact disc-recorder (CD-R) systems, production options changed and replication costs dropped to mere pennies per disc. The system, which consists of a CD-recordable drive and the appropriate software requires a high-capacity, fast hard drive. The large savings in using CD-R as opposed to CD processing makes it economically feasible. The process for producing the CD includes arranging the files, copying the files to hard drive, running performance simulations, and then writing the data to the CD-R disc. If you are interested in making your own CD disc, I recommend the *CD-Recordable Bible* by Dr. Ash Pahwa. It is published by Eight Bit Books. PALINET is an example of a regional network that will contract to produce one-off databases on CD-ROM. The service called PAL/SCAN permits the scanning of reports, books, manuscripts, newsletters, course materials, and anything else printed on paper.

Libraries of all types are producing or planning to produce their own local products. The majority of projects are photo archives or preservation projects or large scale special collections. As production costs continue to drop, other information could be created by the library in CD-ROM format. The Local Government Information Kiosks sprouting up at many libraries, grocery stores, and shopping malls sometimes contain CD-ROM held information locally produced by the library in cooperation with the local government agency.

You have to go fetch the future. It's not coming to you. It's running away .
—Zulu proverb

TECHNOLOGIES CONVERGE TO CREATE VIRTUAL LIBRARIES

What are the elements of a virtual library? There are seven basic components.

1. National and international phone networks or wireless communication paths.
2. Standards and protocols to facilitate linkages. Z39.5 is the standard for interconnectivity. More and more systems are meeting this standard.
3. Automatic, inexpensive digitizing devices.
4. System and human availability. John Naisbitt says in *MegaTrends 2000* that in each step toward technology there must be a balancing emphasis on the personal, individual human element.[12]
5. Copyright, royalty, leasing agreements. Most information companies are building copyright costs and fees into their prices.
6. Commitment to open, no-fee access to the library. If all information is going to cost a fee, then a library isn't a library but rather an information broker raising money from the selling of information. It is particularly important to maintain the commitment to free service in a virtual library as the profession tends to attach fees to most anything that comes through or off a machine.
7. Staff who study public demand and modify the library selection/access policy constantly based on what the users have demanded rather than purchasing materials in anticipation of demand.

Libraries of all types have progressed to containing some elements of a virtual library. One of the earliest attempts was the University of California, Long Beach Library. In the late 1980s, it redid its traditional library. The new library contained a small popular book browse area, plenty of comfortable seating, and row upon row of terminals/workstations connected to the databases and information sources considered by the university library to be most useful and timely. Their further plans to add more terminals and purchase more access were impeded by lack of sufficient funds. For several years their plans slowed but now they are back on track and providing greatly expanded remote access.

The Columbia Law Library's Project Janus is an innovative leap forward to the virtual library. They are using a super computer and highly advanced software. The Law Library is partnering with The Thinking Machine Corporation. This project is unique in that when a question is asked the answer as well as a list of related documents is retrieved. The equipment uses a digital full-text search and retrieves from millions of documents. Currently it is only available to researchers at Columbia but shortly it will be available to outside researchers. In 1996 they will convert 10,000 to 12,000 titles.

Mesa Community College in Phoenix, Arizona, Maricopa Community College District, has created another type of virtual library called the Information Commons. Duane Webster, head of the Association of Research Libraries, at the October 4, 1994 International Video Conference on the Electronic Library, discussed the "Information Commons" concept. He sees the Information Commons as a place where all types of information converge for the easy access of the student. Mesa Community College's goal is to provide a student-driven information environment. In order to meet their goal, they integrated all electronic and print materials to provide a mix of instructional, library, and information related services. The traditional library, the learning resource center, and the computer lab are all merged into the Information Commons. It serves 21,000 students in a 200,000-square-foot center. The Information Commons is sub-divided into three main parts:

1. Maximize on-site access providing eighty-four terminals on-site.
2. Promote remote site access to national and international networks.
3. Access at the single workstation to visual, textual, and audio information.

Howard Community College, a 5,000 student institution in Columbia, Maryland, attempts to ready their students for the information age. "Our students will graduate and face a world where an ability to navigate through the sea of electronic information is a must," said Lucy Gardner, Library Director at Howard Community College. In order to meet the needs of the students, the library provides a collection of network and CD-ROM technologies dubbed the Newsnet. Newsnet is an online system that furnishes the students and researchers with instant access to thousands of journal citations and several hundred thousand full text articles. The system they are using is UMI Power Pages which has at its heart a jukebox that holds 240 CD-ROMs each. The CD-ROM jukeboxes currently store on-site more than 2.2 million exact reproductions of article pages.

Students search and review article abstracts. When they locate an article they want to print, they submit an electronic request. The system locates automatically, then loads, the CD-ROM that contains the article and sends the full image article to the laser printer. Students are notified by an on-screen message that there is a twenty cent per page charge. (This is the same as the cost for photocopies.) Students then pick up their copies at the check-out desk. All of the material in the system has been copyright cleared by UMI. Future plans call for providing access to Newsnet via the campus-wide network so faculty could use the system from their offices.

EBSCOhost's Masterfile Database uses a different approach to provide comprehensive indexing and abstracting for 3,000 journals and the full text of 1,000 titles. EBSCOhost is a complete client-server, Z39.50 compliant, online search and retrieval system. It retrieves digitized information rather than information stored on optical discs. The user-friendly interface and search screens can be custom-adapted for different levels of sophistication on a terminal-by-terminal basis. Accessible through the Internet, it is available on a wide range of hardware platforms.

Libraries which consider themselves practically virtual libraries today are what I have chosen to call blended libraries. They contain the best of the old and the new. In the words of Kenneth Dowlin, Director of the San Francisco Public Library, "The future library is a fortress that has been converted to a pipeline for information transferral."[13]

NOTES

1. Bowers, Richard A. "Making a Business of CD-ROM and Multimedia." Speech. Boston: CD-ROM Expo, October 26, 1993.
2. Martin, Kenneth E. "Elements affecting telecommunications policy." *Rural Libraries* No. 2 (1992):63–64.
3. Tenopir, Carol. "Internet Issues in Reference." *Library Journal* (Oct. 1, 1995):28.

4. McClure, Charles R. *Public Libraries and the Internet: Study Results, Policy Issues, and Recommendations.* Washington, D.C., National Commission on Libraries and Information Services, 1994, p. 3.
5. "Washoe County Library Opens 'Internet Branch'" *Advanced Technology Libraries* (Oct. 1995):2.
6. "New York Public Library on the Web." *LJ Hotline* (Sept. 4, 1995):8.
7. O'Keefe, Steve. "Buy the Book." *Internet World* (June 1995): 59.
8. "Dade County Public Schools Test Technology Intuitively." *LJ Hotline* (May 1) 1995.
9. "The Frequency of the Future." *The Economist* (Sept. 30, 1995) n.p.
10. Personal Interview, Dale Foster, University of South Alabama Library, Mobile, Alabama, 1994.
11. Ramstad, Evan. "Xerox Unveils New All-in-One Office Machines." *The Birmingham News*, (Oct. 13, 1995):5B.
12. Naisbitt, John, and Aburdene, Patricia. *Megatrends 2000.* New York: William Morrow, 1990, p. 298.
13. Carrol, Celia. "Electronic Publishing and Public Libraries." *Information Today* (July/August, 1991):34.

6 TECHNOLOGY WITHOUT TEARS OR WHERE DO I GO FROM HERE?

Poised to take new and different directions, library and information center staff need to create a logical plan to move them from their libraries of today to their libraries of tomorrow. The challenge is to chart and take the next steps without being swept up in the rapids or flooded by the information explosion. You can plan for and make the transition following three basic steps:

1) Demographic review;
2) Keeping abreast of technology and technological change; and
3) writing and constantly reviewing, evaluating, and revising a technology plan.

DEMOGRAPHIC REVIEW

Demography is defined as "the science of vital and social statistics."[1] Planning and community analysis guides recommend that area demographics are the first step in "knowing your community." Books such as *Long Range Planning: a How-To-Do-It Manual for Public Libraries* by Suzanne W. Brenmer and Susan M. Panlatier (Neal/Schuman, 1994) or *Developing a Public Library Collection, Policies and Procedures: A How-To-Do-It Manual for Small and Medium-sized Public Libraries*, by Kay Ann Cassell and Elizabeth Futas (Neal-Schuman, 1991) both have valuable sections on doing community analysis.

TECHNOLOGICAL ASSESSMENT

In addition to the basic statistics about the community the library serves that are necessary for a community profile, in order to prepare a technology plan, other information should be gathered. It is this additional information that will help convince the funding sources you have done your homework before you request money to implement a plan. Start with the national statistics and then try to localize them.

TEN STEPS TO CONDUCTING A TECHNOLOGICAL ASSESSMENT

1—Begin with national statistics on use such as:

- percent of households owning personal computers
- percent of households owning CD-ROM drives
- percent of persons having mobile or cellular phones
- percent of people with personal computers having access to the Internet
- percent of people using personal computers in their daily work
- percent of children using personal computers in school

Some of this information might be obtained from books such as Rand McNally's *Commercial Marketing Business Guide* (1994) which contains a mix of social science and business data.

2. Try to see if any of these statistics are available also for your region or area and compare to the national statistics. In 1995 the Enoch Pratt Free Library (Baltimore, Maryland) discovered from census data that socioeconomic status directly affects who uses computers and how they use them. Therefore, they found that the Information Superhighway was closed to many poor children. Based on this discovery, they designed "A Whole New World: Electronic Information Literacy," a pilot project to train nine- to fourteen-year-olds to communicate with children worldwide through the Internet, to use educational databases, and to improve writing, communication, and comprehension skills.[2]

3. Do a survey of educational institutions in your area and their use of new technologies. Include day care as well as public and private primary, middle, and high schools. Also include any institutions of higher education. Ask if any of these agencies have a technology plan they could share with you.

4. Find out the plans of the local and/or regional telephone provider. Talk to their staff about two things:

a) First, learn about the status of ISDN (Integrated Services Digital Network) service availability. With ISDN you can move voice, data, images, and fax over the same wires. Many phone companies have set up centers where you can check availability in your area. Consult the appropriate source listed in the box on page 100.

About 50 percent of the lines in the United States have

ISDN service. Call the phone company and ask about current coverage as well as plans for the next few years. If they have not planned to provide lines in your area, talk with the person in charge of scheduling lines and explain the importance of an ISDN connection to the library. Remember that in order to take advantage of the increased capabilities of ISDN lines, there must be an ISDN connection at both ends.

b) Determine the phone company's plans to provide interactive television from their company. Since U.S. District Court Judge Sharon Blackburn struck down a provision of the 1984 Cable Act that prohibited telephone companies, such as Bell South, from providing cable television programming in their local telephone service region, it is likely that other phone companies will plan to provide similar service.[3]

5. Learn about the local, municipal, and state governmental agencies' plan to dispense government information. Many states, such as North Carolina, Iowa, and Washington have statewide information distribution networks of some type. If you live in a state with a statewide government information distribution network or with plans for one, you would want your local planning to be consistent with the larger plan.

In many cities and counties, both large and small, it is the city or county government that is initiating an automated distribution system. Sometimes this planning is done without the library as a participant. Volunteer to provide and update community information that could be a value-added segment of a government database. Work to see if your library's catalog can be viewed on the local government information kiosk. Offer the library as a location for the information kiosk. Cite the advantages of evening and weekend availability at the library.

6. Do an inventory of all wireless providers in your area. These will typically be cellular and mobile phone providers. Check television advertising, comb ads in local newspapers, check new phone books under subject headings such as digital equipment, cellular phones, packet switching, wireless communications, and any other new terms that develop.

7. Evaluate the library collection. Determine what percentage of the collection is books, journals, microformat, online, and "other". If you are able, track the percentage of reference requests answered from each format. Clifford Lynch, technology expert from the University of California, has discussed in several recent speeches that access to the journal literature is now on at least the same level (through implementation of abstracting and indexing databases) as access to books. He contends that the balance will continue to shift to increased access to journals. Charting

FIGURE 6.1 Numbers to call for ISDN Information.	
Ameritech:	800 832-6328 Mainly Mid-Western States
AT&T	800 222-7956
Bell Atlantic:	800 570-4736 PA, NY, VA, DE, MD, NJ
BellCore:	800 992-4736 National ISDN Info. Clearinghouse
Bell South:	800 858-9413 NC, SC, GA, FL, AL, MS, TN
GTE:	800 888-8799
MCI:	800 727-5555, 800 995 6505
NYNEX:	800 438-4736 MA, NH, UT, NY, MA, CT, RI
Pacific Telesis:	Nevada Bell 702 333-4811
Pacific Bell:	800 955-0346, 800 472-4736 CA
Southwestern Bell:	800 792 -4736 Austin area
	214 268-1403 Dallas area
	713 576-4300 Houston area
	314 572-0880 Missouri
Sprint:	800 366-2370
U.S. West:	800 898 -9675 WA, OR, ID, MO, WY, ND, SD, NE, MN, IA, CO, UT, AZ, NM

this shift for your library is an important piece of your technology plan.

8. Develop a list of technology stores in your service area in order to understand what equipment and technology people in your area are consuming. Include stores such as office equipment, electronic boutiques, bookstores with computer sections, television sections, and electronic sections of department stores, new product stores such as Sharper Image, video rental stores, phone stores, and video arcades. All of these places use, rent, or sell technology that is used, rented, or purchased by library patrons. These sales outlets also contain equipment and products that could be used by libraries to facilitate information sharing and increase the user-friendliness of library automated systems. Visit these stores and regularly sample their wide range of technological products. Have sales staff demo the products and equipment to you and think if they could possibly have some library application.

When Sony's first small portable book unit came to market in 1991, it was advertised as a portable easy-to-use device for individual book reading (there were ten books available including *Jurassic Park*) and an individual ready reference tool. It was not a commercial success and was taken off the market within a year. It is still used very successfully at libraries in an adaptive use. It is checked out to GED students to encourage their library and reading skills. The Gameboy-like player encourages "playing" with an encyclopedia, something that would not generate excitement with a twenty volume cumbersome, small print, bound paper set.

9. Talk with each cable company that provides service in your area. If you only have one service provider, it is easier for your planning. As mentioned in Chapter 3, cable television companies are competing to be THE information source into homes. They want to use their lines to bring television, telephone, and interactive services directly to customers through only one source—cable television. Some cable firms are changing their names by removing any references to television so the public will begin to view cable companies in an expanded role.

10. Be alert for innovative uses of technology in other parts of your life and see if they could be adapted to library delivery of information. One example of a place one might not expect the newest in technology is a professional baseball park. Interactive Network, as a way of acquainting people with the many features of interactive television, distributes free units for use at professional baseball games. In the small, hand-held unit "In the Dugout," you can test your baseball knowledge by predicting the outcome of each player's at bat and predicting bunt, pitchout, steal/hit, and run statistics. Companies selling interactive television are hoping that individuals will not just want to watch television but to *play* television. They provide the technology to compete live with game shows, solve the mysteries in popular mystery series, and give opinions on news. Could increased and expanded interactivity be helpful in online library catalogs?

Smart card technology offers interesting possible applications for libraries. The smart card computer chip can carry 2 kilobytes of data. With the data fields encoded, this represents a tremendous amount of information. The ATM card used in most banking is a magnetic strip card that includes a numeric identifier which links to a complete record in a centralized database. A smart card is different in that it has the information embedded in the card, not just the connecting link.

The National City Public Library in National City, California participates in a smart card use consortium for The Learning Network. The information on the smart card is the learner's record, a kind of electronic transcript that is transportable by the learner to any of the participating educational agencies. It can be transcribed by any of the agencies. Once a learner is entered into the system, that information would be available from any other entry point on the system.

The Visa Corporation is pursuing a partnership that would put smart cards into its customers' hands, underwriting the encoding costs and providing a part of the memory space on the chip for "community use," a category that could include data helpful to the library patron. It was suggested by Joan Frye Williams of Best-Seller Library Systems at the 1994 Computers in Libraries Conference that a personal interface programmed into a chip on your smart card could provide you with instructions and access codes to any library system to which you had access. The card could include instructions and communications software.[4]

PARTNERSHIPS CAN GROW OUT OF THE DEMOGRAPHIC REVIEW

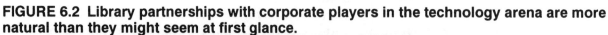

FIGURE 6.2 Library partnerships with corporate players in the technology arena are more natural than they might seem at first glance.

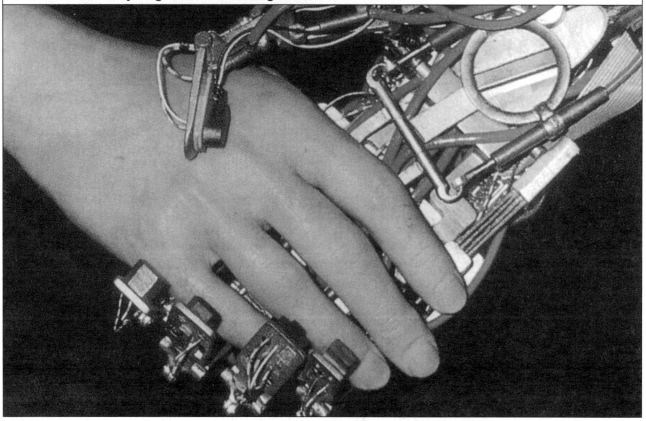

The demographic review stage should also include a view toward potential partnerships. An emerging role for the library is library as partner. Businesses, global entrepreneurs and computer companies are all crossing old borders in search of new partnerships. Mergers and alliances are the highlights of headline news. In partnerships today, perspective mergers are looking for content. Content and knowledge are what libraries can bring to a partnership.

According to Marshall Keyes at an address at the 1994 SOLINET Annual Meeting, there are four goals to a partnership:

1. Be clear about the objectives of the partnership;
2. choose partners that lead to strengths;
3. avoid illusions about partners; and
4. remember that, unlike partnerships in the past, partnerships now are likely to be temporary.

Many libraries that are seeking new partnerships in order to improve services to their clientele are experienced consortiums and/or network members. A recent ad in a library periodical was looking for a partnership consultant who could create and develop library partnerships while able to field test new ideas and promote use by new constituent groups. In library fund raising often new partners are discovered. Be aware that various partners may have different levels of commitment. There are several areas in partnerships that could lead to challenges. Most likely there would be a difference in the corporate culture and the library culture and the absence of a common culture. Each partner may have internal politics of which the other partner is not aware. There easily could be conflicts over the scope of the partnership. There also could be conflicting loyalties. All of these challenges can be overcome, but it is helpful to understand the potential differences when working with partnerships.

There are many joint ventures between libraries and technological firms. In the Library Without a Roof project outlined in Chapter 5, the University of South Alabama Library, a public state institution, worked with three commercial corporations to develop their joint venture.

In the recent past, library automation systems were very proprietary. If you liked one particular feature of a system, rarely could you purchase that feature separately to add to your own system if you were not purchasing the whole system. This purchasing method is changing. Kid's Catalog by CARL can be purchased separately from CARL and added to other online catalog systems. Vendors are also forming alliances and strategic partnerships in order to create and distribute improved, more popular products and technologies. Often, if you approach a vendor regarding a piece of their system or one particular part or feature of it, they will at least talk with you and try to figure out how to provide it to you separately. Computer companies are crossing new borders in the search for new partnerships and partners with clout. The computer industry itself is changing so dramatically that there is no separate computer industry just as there is no single phone company, or one cable industry, or new information industry. There is one big technology industry.

Vendors also are working with individual libraries to develop new products and services. WLN (Washington Library Network), a large western library consortium, worked with the Washington State Department of Wildlife Management to produce a CD-ROM-based wildlife information product to be used as a reference product. Several state libraries are negotiating on behalf of all libraries in their states to provide access to state-held information. There is a multitude of state agencies which collect and store valuable data that would benefit the citizens of a state. Libraries are working on practical methods to providing this access, conveniently and at no cost.

Free-Nets are a significant example of new partnerships. Free-Net is a licensed service mark of the National Public Telecomputing Network Community Service Network. One of the earliest Free-Nets was the Cleveland Free-Net which was set up by Thomas Grunder. The Southeast Library Information Network (SEFLIN) headquartered in Ft. Lauderdale serves an area with 4.5 million people. SEFLIN Free-Net is only two years old but over 200 community groups, agencies, and individuals with special expertise have become their information providers. These community partners are helping to build the information infrastructure in the region. In 1995, 83,631 log-ins were recorded in a single month for just Broward County. SEFLIN Free-Net is also the local on ramp to Internet. The project's future goals include a Spanish language service, a graphical interface, and additional training programs. According to Elizabeth Curry, SEFLIN Executive Director, "The challenge to meet community interest and demand is great but the payoff is equally great with a high level of community involvement."[5]

Technology companies seek out libraries and other information sources to form partnerships. South Central Bell, a Bell South Company, established a partnership with the University of Louisville, South Central Bell, and the Commonwealth of Kentucky. They set up a Kentucky Telecommunications Research Center (TRC) in suburban Louisville. The center offers hands-on experience with the latest educational technology, solutions to business communications problems, information concerning the vital role telecommunications plays in attracting new business, and remote health care access. The center hosted over 25,000 economic developers, educators, and business people in its four-year history. The University of California University System Chancellor's Office came to the library to get expertise, too. University of California Riverside Library Director, Jordan Scepanski, was on special assignment to the chancellor's office to work with the academic computing people to develop new media center communities.

KEEPING ABREAST OF TECHNOLOGY AND TECHNOLOGICAL CHANGE

The second step in planning for transition is keeping abreast of technology and technological change. How can you keep abreast of the swift changes without being overcome? There are five steps that can help:

1. Keep up-to-date. Read and talk.
2. Be on the look out for products and methods that make the libraries' information and resources easier for patrons to use.
3. Take and plan small steps.
4. Continually review policies and procedures.
5. Don't get swept away, stay committed.

STEP ONE: KEEP UP-TO-DATE. READ AND TALK.

All types of media bombard us daily about change and the glories of the information highway. Rather than becoming frustrated, determine the sources that are most productive for you and contain the greatest amount of information that is applicable to your specific situation. These sources could be the traditional library journals. Technology, new product development, and reviews of technology are the focuses of many library magazines. A topical magazine which focuses on a selected technology might be helpful. Because the field is rapidly changing, new magazines continually are published. Often the new titles can be spotted by perusing magazines in bookstores, computer stores, or drug stores. Most magazines will send you a free sample copy. Again, the topical magazines often merge, cease publication, or change title in response to the constantly changing technological market. Journals from related fields often yield helpful information. One example, *Imaging*, aimed at publishers, contains many informative articles that could help in library newsletter printing.

Joining and participating in Internet Listservs can provide interconnectivity with other librarians and information providers which have your same challenges. If you think your technological situation is unique and you want to get ideas and/or possible solutions, pose a question on a Listserv. In keeping current, include reviews of the many excellent books being published by library and non-library presses. Be alert to new titles and review sources that are being developed in response to the ever-changing market. One example is McGraw-Hill's *CD-ROM's Rated: A Guide to the best and worst multimedia titles, 1995.* Until there were enough CD-ROM titles, there would not have been a large book giving quick reviews to help in selection.

STEP TWO: BE ON THE LOOK OUT.

Watch for products and methods that have some applicability to improving service to library patrons. Keep a sharp eye out on the ads in newspapers, magazines, and television. Also, check out weekly columns such as Cyberspace in *Newsweek* which covers technology. Airplane magazines often tout new technological products. The last airline magazine I read would sell me wireless improved speakers for my stereo, a wireless baby watcher that when pinned onto my wandering creeper would help me locate my child anywhere within thirty yards, and a software package that sends street maps covering the metropolitan or national area of my choice to be loaded into my laptop. You key in the address for which you are looking and it places a marker on the exact spot and highlights the best route to get there. The same magazine also described a pen-recognition health care management system which allows home health nurses to quickly gather patient information and to wirelessly transfer this information to doctors. Another ad featured surfing a hot new web site—Newspage, which filters over 15,000 stories from over 500 news sources and categorizes them by topic. Select the topics of interest to you and Newspage goes to work for you. Everyday by 8:00 a.m., you'll receive only those newstories that match your interest. It's amazing to think that all of these products can be found in just one magazine. Perhaps you could put babywatch in your hard-to-secure reference books and you could hone in on their locations with your receiver!

In reading the news, watch for announcements that might affect your library. When the entertainment news announced that Oscar-winning Steven Spielberg was turning his attention from the big screen to the computer screen, children's librarians took note. Spielberg signed a contract to help Knowledge Adventure, Inc. develop educational computer software for children.

As new technology is used in other fields, it becomes both expected and accepted in the library too. Maybe you haven't experienced virtual reality yet but you do go to the dentist. Perhaps the next time you go, you can overcome your dental drill anxiety by donning a pair of Virtual I/Os 3-D eyeglasses. Dental patients can now watch 3-D movies, educational programs, or play video games while sitting in the dentist's chair.

Another area to watch is the newly-emerging network computer market. Several major companies have developed prototypes of the stripped-down, $500-range, network computer. The bells and whistles found on $3,000 PCs are often not fully utilized by average users. This new computer essentially would serve as a laptop window to the World Wide Web. Eric Schmidt, Sun Microsystems' Chief Technical Officer said, "This is the next stage in the development of the Net."[6] Consider the vast difference in the number of people who could afford a $500 computer versus those who could afford to spend $3,000. Consider also the number of public access terminals a library could provide if each one only cost $500. The development of such a basic computer which provided network access is one that librarians should carefully monitor as it will have a significant effect on home access to information as well as a method of providing affordable public access to Internet access in libraries.

Trends in the development of television often have an impact on libraries and computers. Two recent technological developments will have an impact on the equipment purchased for libraries. As television manufacturers continue to work toward affordable higher-definition television, this work is affecting the shape of the high-resolution computer monitors. Sony has a high-end unit with a 28" diagonal viewing area capable of displaying, crisply, three letter-sized pages side by side. Although the large screen is not economically feasible for libraries yet, its development should be followed. Seventeen-inch computer monitors have dropped in price significantly and several companies have the larger screen available.

Convergent technologies make it possible for you to watch television on your computer screen or add computer features to your television. Monitor new commercial television developments and compare these to your current information delivery methods. The multifunctional PC has been dubbed an information appliance.

While you are on the look out for new products and methods of information delivery, consider a trip to a virtual theme park or virtual entertainment complex. One such center is the Cinetropolis at Foxwood, Connecticut, a casino owned by the Mashantucket Pequot tribe. The Cinetropolis is not much bigger than a supermarket but contains four different kinds of cinema experiences, clustered around shops and restaurants. One cinema shows feature films projected at high resolution on a giant sixty feet screen.

Another provides virtual-reality adventure. A third has 360 degree projection and ear-shattering surround sound. The fourth theater is a "turbo tour" theater that offers military-style flight simulators. Unlike fixed attractions or rides in a theme park, Cinetropolis attractions are reprogrammable. They plan to change it three times a year.[7]

Blockbuster Entertainment launched a string of adult "block party" entertainment complexes which feature some of the most complex virtual reality. Included in their 50,000 square feet complex are 3D games, full immersion VR systems, including a turbo-ride moving theater that sways, rumbles, and shakes in sync to the ride's full motion video.[8]

Your next trip after coming back to earth from your virtual breathtaking roller coaster ride should be to the nearest mega-bookstore computer department. Study the room arrangement, lighting, methods of displaying the various products and equipment for public use, and observe the instruction and help from staff. Spend several hours there to determine what people are looking for and the questions they ask. See if there are any ideas you can apply to your library.

STEP THREE: TAKE AND PLAN SMALL STEPS.

Although it might be desirable to implement your entire technological vision at one time, it probably isn't feasible. You may have cost constraints, staff constraints, space constraints, or all of the above. Take your plan and divide it into very small parts. Then divide those parts again. Even if you are able to only implement the first small step, you are on your way. The board and your co-workers will not feel as threatened if you begin with small pieces that will get you to the final, larger goal. If you are able to finish several of the smaller steps, your feeling of accomplishment will be greater and the momentum for your project will naturally increase.

Consider doing something as simple as circulating CD-ROMs. The Geauga County Public Library in Chardon, Ohio tried this successfully. Beginning in 1994 the library already was in the CD-ROM reference business and the music CD loaning business. The staff designed a survey to determine what type of equipment their users owned and which subject areas materials were wanted. Based on the overwhelming response from the public the staff decided " . . . to add new formats more quickly than in the past."[9] This is an example of a small but positive step in implementing technological change.

FIGURE 6.3 A Circulating CD-ROM Collection

STEP FOUR: CONTINUAL REVIEW OF POLICIES AND PROCEDURES.

In the Geauga County experience, the library found that its existing policy did not cover purchase of the CD-ROM formats. Some libraries have updated their policies to include words such as "all types and formats" so that they do not have to continually revise the policies every time they purchase a new format.

There are many policy and procedure questions that need to be addressed when the library starts providing public access to the Internet. The Seattle Public Library took an early lead in this area. It has revised its policy several times. Factors to consider when developing policies are:

1. *Workstation traffic.* After interviewing more than twenty-four university librarians, Carol Tenopir, a professor in the School of Library and Information Science at the University of Tennessee-Knoxville, concluded that

"No matter how many workstations and dial-up ports a library plans, more will likely be needed as the word spreads and the popularity of online services increases."[10]

You might consider sign-up sheets and express stations for quick reference. Many workstation congestion problems are similar to those experienced when online catalogs were first introduced. The service is inherently popular because it is new. Some libraries introduce new services to the public even when those services are under-configured as a way of building increased budget support. If you choose this tack, try to find some way of adding more workstations in order to maintain credibility.

2. *Games and Chat.* E-mail is one of the more frequently used features of Internet access through libraries. Interactive virtual games and other chat activities are popular. Some librarians think that these are not legitimate uses of library-sponsored access lines and develop policies which prohibit such uses. Some of these same librarians have not bought video games for patrons deeming them frivolous. Some library staff have blocked patron access to games found on online services and they don't allow patrons to bring in their own games to play on library computers. Many normally non-library people will become attracted to the library if you offer e-mail access.

3. *Difficulty of Monitoring Adherence to Restrictive Policies.* Unless you have a full-time programmer who can develop blocking mechanisms or extra staff to roam past workstations every fifteen minutes to determine what people are accessing, try to write fairly non-restrictive policies. It might be easier to set a time limit on terminal use instead of trying to look of users' shoulders. Librarians in all types of settings grapple with policy and procedure issues since the Internet is a medium which inherently encourages exploration, discovery, finding new paths, experimentation, and creativity. Just like school children thirty years ago could be found snickering over the sex words in their new dictionary, some children today have found access points to questionable material on the Internet. Keep abreast of the legal issues concerning public access to sexually explicit materials.

Often procedures also will need to be revised. If your library decides to order books from one of the 300 booksellers on the Internet, it probably would require a change in procedure. "The Access to Electronic Information Services and Networks: an Interpretation of the Library Bill of Rights" was written by the ALA Intellectual Freedom Committee. Although not yet formally adopted by the ALA Council, it addresses many issues including economic barriers to access and collection development. Each library needs to consider its own policies of access, including access to children of electronic formats.

STEP FIVE: DON'T GET SWEPT AWAY, STAY COMMITTED.

Technology change can feel like glacier melt. The snow melts swiftly, at unpredictable times, and floods the surrounding rivers and sometimes the surrounding countryside. So too does the amount of and demand for new technology swell the demands on our library budget. Glacier melt disperses and flows on to sustain thousands of smaller connected rivers. New technology ebbs and flows also and eventually evens out to be a supportive, helpful force. During times that seem like glacier melt, stay committed. Before beginning a digital library initiative, you will need to make sure that the library's information foundation is firm and that staff and patrons have adequate tools for the service capabilities. If you already have an automated online catalog and one or more workstations connected to a local area network, review the following suggestions made by Richard Luce, project leader of The Library Without Walls and Director of the Research Library for the Los Alamos National Laboratory. Keep focused and remember the emerging technologies continuum.

In order to lay a strong, robust technology foundation, determine where your library is in:

1. *Upgrading the online catalog.* Many librarians, staff, board members, school principals, and college deans think that automating the catalog is a once-in-a-lifetime job. Evaluate the existing catalog for the following capabilities:
   a) Easy connection to the Internet
   b) Ability to load external databases
   c) Capacity to serve an ever-increasing number of simultaneous users
   d) Ability to be accessed externally
2. *Modernizing the Workstation Toolset*
   a) Provide fully-connected terminals for support staff
   b) Ability of desktop workstations to access library systems

        c) Connect workstations to both internal and external networks
3. *Developing a robust local area network*
        a) Integration of workstations with CD-ROM databases
        b) Access to Internet resources
        c) Electronic mail to facilitate communications
        d) Shared application software[11]

According to Rob McGee, noted automation consultant, in a 1995 speech to the New Hampshire Library Association, "The problem for communities with libraries that do not have adequate information technology is: the longer they wait, the further behind they get. And the more the opportunities the public loses to enter the digital world!!"[12] Don't get swept away in the glacier melt. There can be technology without tears.

DEVELOPING A TECHNOLOGY PLAN WITHOUT SHEDDING TEARS

This next section will discuss factors which are unique to basic technological planning. For detailed information on writing a plan refer to any of the many excellent planning guides available. After that general review, concentrate on the part that will be your technological plan. Determine the method you will use, who will be involved, and whether you will use a survey. If you are a single person library, this stage may consist of you sitting down at your desk writing and developing the plan.

The demographic review/technological assessment stage should yield information such as:

- how many workers work at home;
- what equipment is owned by people in your service area;
- the major technology-related industries in your area;
- information about those company's workforces; and
- school media center technology—existing and planned.

The technology plan should consider several major areas outlined in the box below:

FIGURE 6.4 Element of a technology plan

Library Mission
Introduction—short several paragraphs; a statement about current technology use in the library
Goals—sample areas for goals
- Circulation—internal staff goals, automated services goals
- Access point—hours accessible, how accessible
- Collections—electronic resources
- Connectivity (internal and external)
- Facilities
- Staff and Community involvement
Objectives—including job tasks and dates
Costs—sources of funding, grants
Equipment—type and location
Hardware and software configuration diagrams
Security and disaster plan

New technologies make sense only when the cost of maintaining the existing system is higher than the cost of installing and maintaining a new system. A plus to the new technologies is the added value of the services the new system will bring to the patrons and staff, but this is not the only issue.

Several differences exist between writing a library long-range plan and writing a technology plan. Due to the fast pace of technological change, most technical plans are written to cover a one-to-three-year cycle. It is difficult to anticipate the cost of an automation plan. The costs of both equipment and connectivity change quickly, often downward. If you have three years between your cost estimates and the time you purchase the equipment, you probably will be able to purchase additional equipment for the same cost or more advanced equipment. If the plan is a three-year plan, review it in detail every six months and revise it frequently as needed. Technology plans cover a short cycle, they are difficult to cost out, and they require frequent revision and review. The goals for the San Francisco Public Library's Automation Department shown in the following box exemplify a model plan which recognizes and deals with these issues.

FIGURE 6.5 Sample San Francisco Public Library Automation Department Goals

Mission

The San Francisco Public Library System is dedicated to free and equal access to information, knowledge, and the joys of reading for our diverse community.

Department Goals Over the Next Three Years

Information Systems

The San Francisco Public Library over the last few years has focused on developing and constructing an information system foundation that will take us into the next century. The Library will be seen as the source for all types of information that relate directly to both the traditional mission of a library and non-traditional services and serve as a community resource for all types of consumer information. The following long range goals were adopted by the Library Commission and reflect systemwide importance of a strong information system program.

System Access

Over the next five years, SFPL will find the means to have open each of the twenty-six neighborhood branches and the main library at least sixty hours per week, with computer access available twenty-four hours a day. It will achieve stable and adequate funding which will ensure attainment of the strategic goals and service levels.

Collections

The Public Library will develop and maintain a body of books, materials, and electronic resources reflecting San Francisco's diversity, suitable for its contemporary needs, and providing for its future vitality. The Public Library will double the size of its book collections within fifteen years, with an immediate goal of adding one new book per child each year.

In addition to its broad-based general collection, the Public Library will focus special attention on those services of particular importance to the community, such as services for children, the sight and hearing impaired, small business development, adult literacy, health information, and community based organizations.

Where there is a serious need and interest, the Public Library will develop a few special collections suitable for in-depth research, inviting scholarly inquiry and community participation and support.

Facilities

The Public Library's facilities will be fully functional; conducive to reading, learning, and thought; and supported by state-of-the-art, easy-to-use technology.

Community Pride

The Public Library will be a source of pride for the people of San Francisco as a resource for individual and community achievement, as a democratic institution, and bastion of intellectual freedom, as an asset for the literacy community, and as a focal point for civic, community, and neighborhood activity. Every child in San Francisco will have a Public Library card.

Staff and Community Involvement

The Public Library's staff will be diverse, personable, helpful, professional, and fully capable of meeting a broad spectrum of needs. The staff will have the expertise required to collect, preserve, organize, and disseminate information and knowledge. The library will provide its staff with the atmosphere, training, and resources necessary for personal development; and will provide the public with access to a trained and professional staff. The Public Library will encourage community participation in the institution, recruiting a large number of talented advisers, scholars, docents, fund-raisers, and volunteers to support and enhance library services.

A large library leader in the integrated use of technology, San Francisco Public Library's online resources range from full text literary classics to medical research, to news articles with the current financial information, to tips on how to prepare for an earthquake. Which existing equipment you will keep and what you will trade or discard will be part of your plan. Trade and discard without regret. Most equipment is used many additional years than originally projected.

The critical factor in writing your plan is your local situation. Consider answers to these questions. What will be most helpful to the patrons you serve? Will the planned technology improve the quality of the patron's research? Will it help the patrons get the information they need more quickly, easily, conveniently, and in an easy-to-understand way? Do your patrons need text only or graphics, audio, and interactivity? How current does the information need to be? You and your staff and teachers or board members can best answer these questions and factor the answers into the technology plan.

When trying to make decisions about hardware selection, the important factor to remember is that hardware changes daily. No matter how carefully you select the particular equipment to meet the library's needs, there always will be something better coming to market. Going into the selection process knowing these two facts will avoid the "I should have waited" or "I didn't make the right selection."

Easy Internet navigational tools and the availability of the Internet to the library's patrons when you make your equipment selection will have profound effects on choices you make in the automation process. Keep current on the most recent information on Internet usage as it is constantly changing. The Internet will affect the smallest libraries the most because it provides an opportunity for more information, regardless of the size of the institution. As Dr. Stephan S. Wolff, Head of Networking with the National Science Foundation, said about the emerging network, "You can be physically isolated without being intellectually isolated."

NOTES

1. *Random House Dictionary of the English Language.* New York: Random House, 1969, p. 384.
2. "Children See New World," *Public Libraries* (October 1995):269.
3. Singleton, William C. "Bell South Going Interactive" *Birmingham Post-Herald* (October 1, 1995):5E
4. Nelson, Nancy Melin. "Smart Librarians: Smart Cards." *Information Today* (April 1994):17.
5. Curry, Elizabeth. "Expanding SEFLIN Free-Net." *SEFLIN Exchange* vol 6 #1 (Spring 1995):2.
6. "Computers: A $500 Net Box?" *Newsweek* (October 2, 1995):n.p.
7. "Theme Parks; Feeling the future" *The Economist* (Feb. 1994):74.
8. Dysart, Joe. "Not just kid's stuff anymore" *VR World* (May/June 95):22–23.
9. Lubelski, Greg. "Multimedia to go: circulating CD-ROMs at Geauga County Public Library" *Library Journal* (February 1, 1995):39.
10. Tenopir, Carol. "Internet Issues in Reference." *Library Journal* (October 1, 1995):28.
11. Luce, Richard E. "Shaping the Library of the Future: Digital Library Developments at the Los Alamos National Laboratory's Research Library." Paper presented at Infotech '94. October 25–26, 1994, Oak Ridge, Tennessee, p.3.
12. McGee, Rob, 1995. Speech delivered to New Hampshire Library Association.

7 THE CHALLENGE OF IMPLEMENTING CHANGING TECHNOLOGIES

"The library of the future will not be an isolated collection of books. It will, on the contrary, be a unit in a great network. Any book in any library anywhere will be available to the most remote reader in the farther-most ends of the country."[1] This description of the library of the future penned by Senator Lister Hill of Alabama in 1957 was contained in an address to the Friends of the Tuscaloosa Public Library. Almost forty years ago the proud sponsor of the Library Services Act envisioned libraries as connecting points to reach out for the world's knowledge. Senator Hill went on to say, " . . . a new horizon is opening up for the librarian of the library of the future. The challenges and opportunities seem to be almost unlimited."[2]

What are other people saying about the challenges of libraries and librarians in the future?

— James Swan, Central Kansas Library System Administrator, "If they (Libraries) hold on to the past without implementing technology, they will find themselves with a shrinking constituency. If they embrace technology at the expense of traditional services, they could lose old customers without recruiting new ones. The challenge for the library in the 1990s is to take advantage of new opportunities, without losing sight of traditional values that have made public libraries so popular. . . . We have to have the courage to build bridges between the present and the future."[3]

— Paul Saffo, Institute of the Future, "The future belongs to neither conduit or content players, but to those who control filtering, searching, and sense-making tools that we rely on through the expanse of cyberspace."[4]

— "Maybe I'm wrong, but I should say that in ten years textbooks as the principal methods of teaching will be as obsolete as the horse and buggy carriage are now. I believe that in the next ten years visual information—the imparting of exact information through the motion picture camera—will be a matter of course in all our schools. . . . Books are clumsy methods of instruction at best and even the words of explanation in them have to be explained."[5] Thomas Alva Edison

— Ward Shaw, CARL Corporation, "Librarians need to change their collecting focus. They can no longer focus on the "back room"... . They cannot focus on the physical collection itself nor on political jurisdiction and competition. Users simply want information . . . Librarians must provide users with advice and critical support; they must figure out how to connect end users to the information they need easily and seamlessly. They must use disparate systems efficiently. Their goal should be to deliver results, be they documents, photographs, or sounds, in a precisely targeted, transparently useful, and affordable manner."[6]

— Clarence R. Graham, 1949, "Libraries and librarians are still in the middle ages. Unless we bring ourselves up-to-date . . . we are going to be really obsolete."[7]

— Paul Evan Peters, Executive Director, Coalition for Networked Information, "Our role is clear. Libraries and people who work in them must become proficient at using their experience to help their communities provide access to a facility with Information Age concepts, techniques and methods."[8]

— Brian Kelley, Director of Palm Beach Community College, "As we stand at the beginning of a new era of information access and resource sharing, it seems to me that the challenges facing up to us are the same facing Edward R. Murrow more than 3 decades ago. [It] [TV] can teach, it can illuminate. Yes, and it can even inspire. But it can do so only to the extent that humans are determined to use it to these ends. Otherwise it is just lights and wires in a box. It is up to us to lead the way, to inspire, to somehow find a way to continue the most important job of librarians—provide free access to information regardless of what form it may be in . . . The challenges are to implement our network and fulfill its enormous potential while also promoting reading, books and other services . . . to make our libraries more than lights and wires in a box."[9]

— Dagmar Koch, Director of Library Systems Worldwide for McDonald Information Systems, "Tomorrow's system must be planned and structured in different ways. We must build systems that can satisfy the needs of today's libraries and move beyond to be able to accommodate the potential requirements of the future."[10]

— "Instead of a rich emporium of literature and wisdom for the ages, the electronic library has turned into Wal-mart, a showroom of products intended for quick sale and rapid replacement—the epitome of mass culture."[11] Nicholson Baker

Cheryl LaGuardia, Coordinator of the Electronic Teaching Center, Harvard College Library, clearly sums up the library's future as follows: "Successfully combining print with electronic collections in the real library calls for vigorous collaboration among the major players creating and using information and information systems: librarians, publishers, and library researchers. All three groups have a vital stake in the creation of future research systems—all three must be intimately involved in the process of finding research systems that deliver information in optimal formats if research and scholarship programs are to progress and flourish."[12]

As alternative scenarios for tomorrow's library proliferate, each librarian and library media specialist should review his or her local situation, then pick and choose which pieces make sense for the library's planning and future. How you arrange the lights and wires in your box is your choice. You are the one most qualified to make the decisions. As you make the most of technological changes monitor the following trends:

1) New partnerships formed to develop improved information products. One example of this is Silver Platter's partnership with Ameritech Library Services, UMI, and publishing partners around the globe to add Silver Platter's collection of databases to their services. Another example is the partnership between Matrix Publishing Network and British Telecom, which will provide unprecedented connectivity, enough to support full multimedia including sound and video. This partnership offers new billing and encryption technologies, which provides the security that is necessary to transact business over the Internet. Another result of this joint venture is that Matrix offers a consulting service to assist authors, libraries, and businesses in putting their documents quickly onto the Internet.

2) A lifetime phone number is a phone number assigned much as a social security number which would follow you for life. It is being offered using a 500 area code.

3) Computer, telecommunications, and software giants will all make a significant entrance into the information services market. These companies have the resources to experiment and will bring radically different approaches, perspectives, and entirely new products.

4) OCLC will continue to work toward building a searchable database of bibliographic records for Internet-accessible materials. An increasing number of OCLC services will be available on the Internet.

5) Interface Improvement. As vendor competition increases, more improvements will be available on the interface,

the part of software that helps users decide what, how, and where to search.

6) More databases and more users. Many libraries and organizations have built a database that could be of interest to a third party. The Internet provides a method for others to access these databases. Based on annual subscription growth rates, it is anticipated that there will be a 20 percent annual growth rate for subscribers to electronic information. That would mean that by 1999, there would be approximately 7.5 million users.[13] As costs continue to drop, more individuals will be able to afford the service.

7) Changes in the Internet. Unless it continues to be easier to use the Internet, people could become disillusioned. However, there are numerous products and services that improve Internet access for the end user. It is unclear how the Internet will continue to deal with the burgeoning number of users and the slowdown in access speed this causes. The library's role in providing Internet information will continue to be defined. Despite all these unknowns Internet service and access will continue to have a profound effect on all types and sizes of libraries.

8) Telephone long distance charges will be minimal and not distance-dependent. This change could have a profound effect on global communications.

Each of these trends directly affects library service and library technology planning as illustrated in the following chart.

FIGURE 7.1   Potential Library Effects of Current Trends

Trend	Possible Library Effect
1. New partnerships	- Improved information products available - New players entering the library market - New jobs in libraries for partnering consultants - Each partner brings unique, new assets to joint ventures
2. Lifetime phone numbers	- Ease of people connecting with each other - Ease of reaching people - Potential for the phone to be a more important mechanism for information delivery
3. New, gigantic players in the information market	- Certain technologies will gain market dominance - Increased globalization - Potential for cost reductions - Possible new delivery methods
4. OCLC increasing Internet services	- Ease of access expanding - More direct access for businesses and individuals - Increased competition with others in information provision
5. Interface improvement	- Product acceptance increasing as ease of use improves - More people willing to try technology - Staff acceptance increasing
6. More database, more users	- More demand for access - Increased mass storage requirements - Potential cost-reduction due to increased competition - Expanded demand for services - Higher patron expectations
7. Changes in the Internet	- Patrons more knowledgeable and more accepting - Patrons more demanding - Traditional library users find information themselves and bypass the library - More dependence on the Internet as a library reference source
8. Telephone Costs Nosedive	- Global reference service becomes a reality - Online services are reconfigured - All communications-dependent industries and products change dramatically

RAPIDS OF CHANGE

Technology provides libraries and librarians with fascinating possibilities and opportunities. As we move down the rapids of change, use what you have learned from past experience, don't be overwhelmed, and enjoy.

> *We live in the rapids of change. The white waters carry us quickly on; we cannot slow down the changes coming to our culture, our society, our families, ourselves. But we do have a choice: we can learn to enjoy turbulence rather than be overwhelmed by it.*
> —Robert Theobald

NOTES

1. Hill, Lister. "The Library of the Future" *Alabama Librarian* no 3 Vol. 8 (July, 1957):52.
2. Hill, "The Library of the Future," p. 52.
3. Swan, James. "The Future of Libraries." *Marigold Library System Newsletter.* (November 1994):13.
4. Lunin, Lois. "Digital Look." *Information Today* (Feb. 1995):33.
5. Edison, Thomas Alva. *The Diary and Sundry Observations of Thomas Alva Edison.* Philosophical Library, 1948, 37.
6. Commentary, *Advanced Technologies/Libraries* (March, 1995):9.
7. Graham, Clarence R. "Are Libraries Obsolete" *The Alabama Librarian.* vol 1 #1 (Dec 1949):4.
8. Peters, Paul Evan. "Information Age Aviators." *Library Journal,* (March 15, 1995):34.
9. Kelley, Brian. "My vision: More than Lights and Wires in a Box" *SEFLIN Exchange* (Winter 1995):5.
10. Koch, Dagmar. "New Horizons for Information Systems." *Library Association Record.* (September 1994):6.
11. Baker, Nicholson. "The Trashing of America's Great Libraries." *The New Yorker* (April 4, 1994):201.
12. LaGuardia, Cheryl. "Virtual Dreams Give Way to Digital Reality." *Library Journal* (Oct. 1, 1995):44.
13. Miller, Tim. "Online in 1994: Ten Predictions." *Information Today* (Nov. 1994):55.

INDEX

COLOPHON

Kathleen R.T. Imhoff is the Assistant Director of Broward County Library in Fort Lauderdale, Florida. An M.L.S. graduate of the University of Wisconsin-Madison, she is a well-known lecturer, writer, workshop leader, technology innovator, and change agent.

Having worked as a director in small, rural libraries, a medium-sized library, a state library agency, and major urban libraries, she brings a unique perspective to managing technology in all types of libraries. She was an early proponent of the improved patron service offered by roll-microfiche, facsimile, CD-ROM technology, inter-library networking, and partnering.

As the first project coordinator for SEFLIN (Southeast Florida Library Information Network), she helped expand access to the four million people of the South Florida region by improving, automating, and speeding delivery of information among all types of libraries.

An active member of state, regional, national, and international library associations, she has served two terms as Councilor of the American Library Association, was a member of the John Cotton Dana Committee, President of the Public Relations Section, and twice President of the Public Library System Section of the Public Library Association.

Kathleen R.T. Imhoff was a recipient of the ALA/PLA/CLSI International Study Award, recipient of the Bumblebee Cannot Fly Award, President of the Leadership Shelby Alumni Group, and is a dedicated advocated for improving library services to all.

Additional Titles of Interest

THE INTERNET ACCESS COOKBOOK:
A Librarian's Commonsense Guide to Low-Cost Connections
by Karen G. Schneider

"What distinguishes this title from the glut of Internet books in print is its ability to empower a computer novice with the knowledge and confidence to successfully plan and connect to the Internet. Schneider, *American Libraries*' 'Internet Librarian' columnist . . . covers everything. This is recommended. Bon appetit!" *Library Journal*

1-55570-235-X. 1995. 6 x 9.
322 pp. $24.95.

USING THE WORLD WIDE WEB AND CREATING HOME PAGES:
A How-To-Do-It Manual for Librarians
by Ray E. Metz and Gail Junion-Metz

The first and only manual specifically designed to help you browse the Web, *Using the World Wide Web and Creating Home Pages* demonstrates how to integrate the Web into your library services, and build a home page for your library that will be the toast of the electronic community.

1-55570-241-4. 1996. 8 1/2 x 11.
200 pp. $45.00.

REFERENCE AND COLLECTION DEVELOPMENT ON THE INTERNET:
A How-To-Do-It Manual for Librarians
By Elizabeth Thomsen

Here is a cutting-edge manual that evaluates and gives librarians the tools to find thousands of different Internet resources that offer guidance in collection development and reference services. It explains how and where to benefit from online communities, e-mail professional interest groups, Usenet newsgroups, literary groups, FAQs, and electronic texts.

1-55570-243-0. 1996. 8 1/2 x 11.
240 pp. $45.00.

FINDING GOVERNMENT INFORMATION ON THE INTERNET:
A How-To-Do-It Manual
Edited by John Maxymuk

"For librarians and anyone else with interest in government information policy, this book offers the most comprehensive overview available of government information on the Internet . . . thorough and well-documented . . . " *Library Journal*

1-55570-228-7. 1996. 8 1/2 x 11.
264 pp. $45.00.

USING THE INTERNET, ONLINE SERVICES, AND CD-ROMs FOR WRITING RESEARCH AND TERM PAPERS
Edited by Charles Harmon

This unique guide is a basic, comprehensive manual for high school and college students that does for electronic resources what Turabian does for print. Includes MLA and APA citation formats for Internet and CD-ROM sources.

1-55570-238-4. 1996. 6 x 9.
170 pp. $29.95.

THE CD-ROM PRIMER: THE ABC'S OF CD-ROM
By Cheryl LaGuardia

"LaGuardia is writing for both the home and professional user, and her coverage of the field features the latest in multimedia products . . . [she] touches all the CD-ROM bases . . . in this recommended title." *Library Journal*

" . . . a good summary of the current state of CD-ROM technology and a glimpse into the future development of the technology . . . [LaGuardia] gives sound advice on how to evaluate multimedia needs and test-drive multimedia hardware and software . . . beginners to CD-ROM technology may find *The CD-ROM Primer* a useful way to ease into . . . multimedia." *Library Software Review*

1-55570-167-1. 1994. 8 1/2 x 11.
250 pp. $45.00.

TECHNOLOGY AND COPYRIGHT LAW:
A Guidebook for the Library, Research, and Teaching Professions
by Arlene Bielefeld and Lawrence Chesseman

This groundbreaking guide—designed and written for non-lawyers—will help you avoid and respond appropriately to difficulties stemming from electronic copyright. Part I covers history and trends for the future, including the probable effects of recommendations from the National Information Infrastructure Report. Part II explores technology and copyright in libraries and classrooms, focusing on fair use doctrine, broadcasting, duplication and distribution, first sale doctrine, and contractual agreements. Part III offers information on copyright law and the electronic classroom, networks, and international agreements.

1-55570-267-8. 1996. 6 x 9.
150 pp. $49.95.

FOUNDATIONS OF FULL TEXT ELECTRONIC INFORMATION DELIVERY SYSTEMS:
Implications for Information Professionals
By Harry M. Kibirige

Here is a readable, broad-reaching discussion of the isses—and problems—of electronic full text information delivery and its technological foundations, authored by a leading expert in the field. Both tutorial and analytical, this volume is required reading for information professionals who want the most up-to-date research in this important area.

1-55570-208-2. 1996. 6 x 9.
350 pp. $45.00.

LOCAL AREA NETWORKING FOR THE SMALL LIBRARY:
A How-To-Do-It Manual for Librarians, 2nd edition
By Norman Howden

Librarians who want to know when to implement and how to work with LAN technology will find guidance in this clear explanation that covers every aspect of LAN—from start-up through maintenance and trouble shooting. The second edition has been updated to include information on CD-ROM networks, steps for making the Internet and the Web accessible via the LAN, tips on setting up employee and public user workstations, and more.

Praise for the 1st edition:

" . . . enthusiastically and knowledgeably written . . . " *Library Journal*

" . . . equivalent to having the advice of an experienced LAN consultant." *Computers in Libraries*

1-55570-104-3. 1996. 8 1/2 x 11.
147 pp. $35.00.

IMNPLEMENTING AN AUTOMATED CIRCULATION SYSTEM:
A How-To-Do-It Manual
By Kathleen G. Fouty

Here is a comprehensive how-to designed to take readers at all libraries through the complicated process of installing a new automated circulation system or software program, step-by-step. Topics covered include a history of circulation automation, its advantages and limitations, the role of the project manager, working with the system software and hardware, converting library records, examining policies and procedures, staff training, publicity and user training, and evaluation.

" . . . excellent . . . will help anyone charged with implementing an automated circulation system." *Booklist*

1-55570-175-2. 1994. 8 1/2 x 11.
232 pp. $39.95.

PLANNING FOR AUTOMATION:
A How-To-Do-It Manual for Librarians
By John M. Cohn, Ann L. Kelsey, and Keith Michael Fiels

" . . . the authors have done an excellent job of concentrating on the essentials . . . recommended for those responsible for planning automation projects in small or medium-sized libraries or for use as a workbook in a library automation course." *Online*

"well-organized . . . an essential purchase for all professional collections." *Library Journal*

"If you haven't automated yet and you plan to do so in the near future, read this book." *Computers in Libraries*

1-55570-120-5. 1992. 8 1/2 x 11.
128 pp. $42.50.

Publication dates, prices, and number of pages for new titles may be estimates and are subject to change.

To order or request further information, contact:
Neal-Schuman Publishers
100 Varick Street, New York, NY 10013
212-925-8650
or fax toll free—1-800-584-2414